KEEP OFF THE GRASS

KEATON

ℛℛ

Ravette London

This book is dedicated to Michael Joseph Duff

First published by Ravette Limited, 1987
© Ravette Limited 1987

Printed and bound in Great Britain
for Ravette Limited,
3 Glenside Estate, Star Road, Partridge Green
Horsham, Sussex RH13 8RA
by The Guernsey Press Company Limited,
Guernsey, Channel Islands

ISBN 1 85304 015 0

For the joy and the colour
   That comes from your plot
Thank God in his wisdom
   He thought of the lot!

For the back you've just broken
   From mowing and toil
Blame that chap Adam
   First man of the soil!

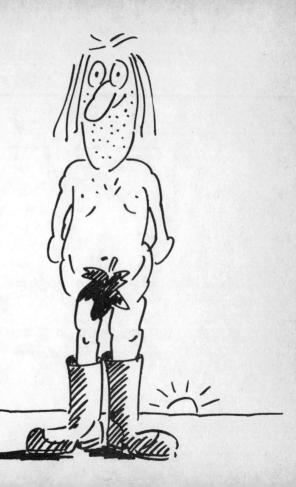

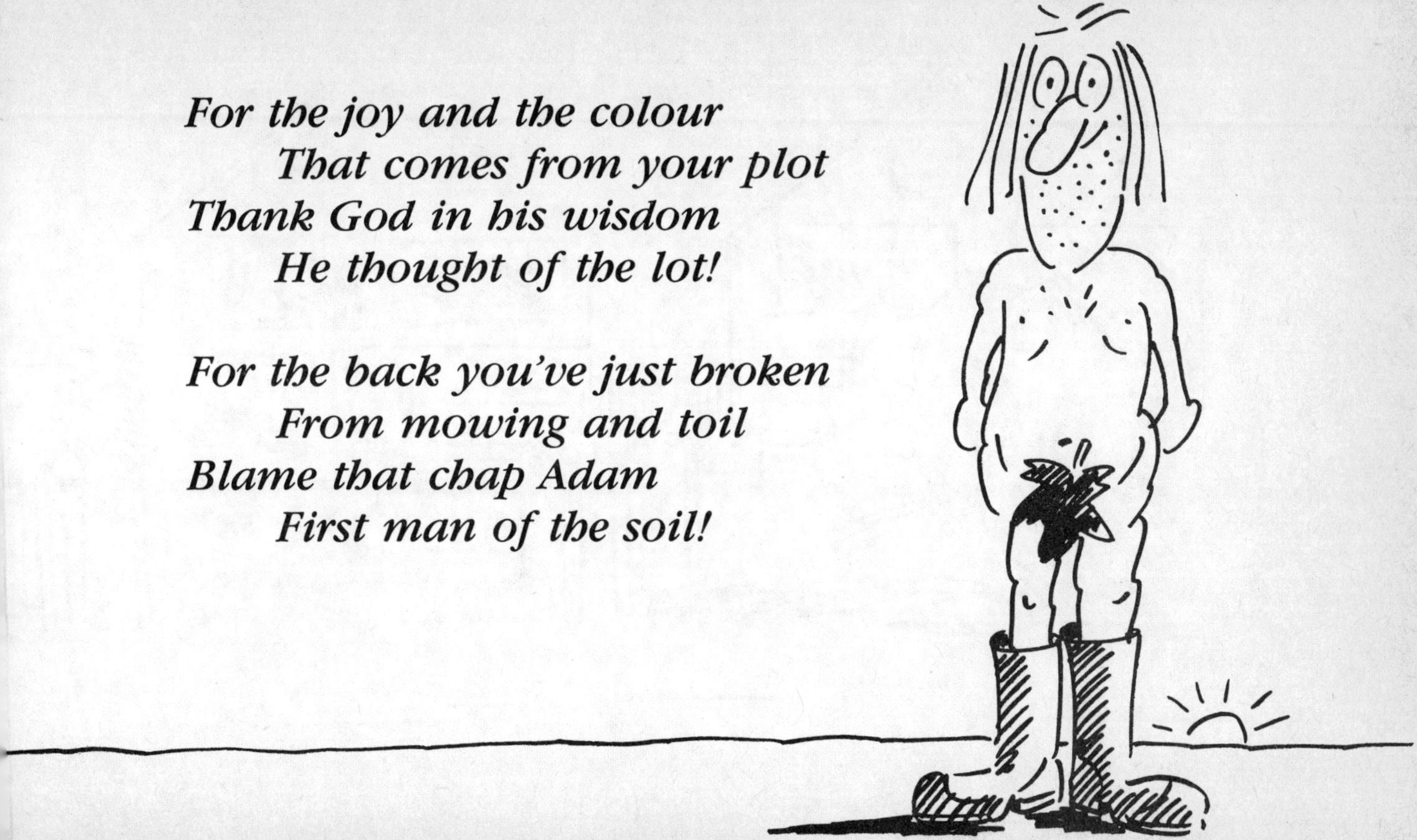

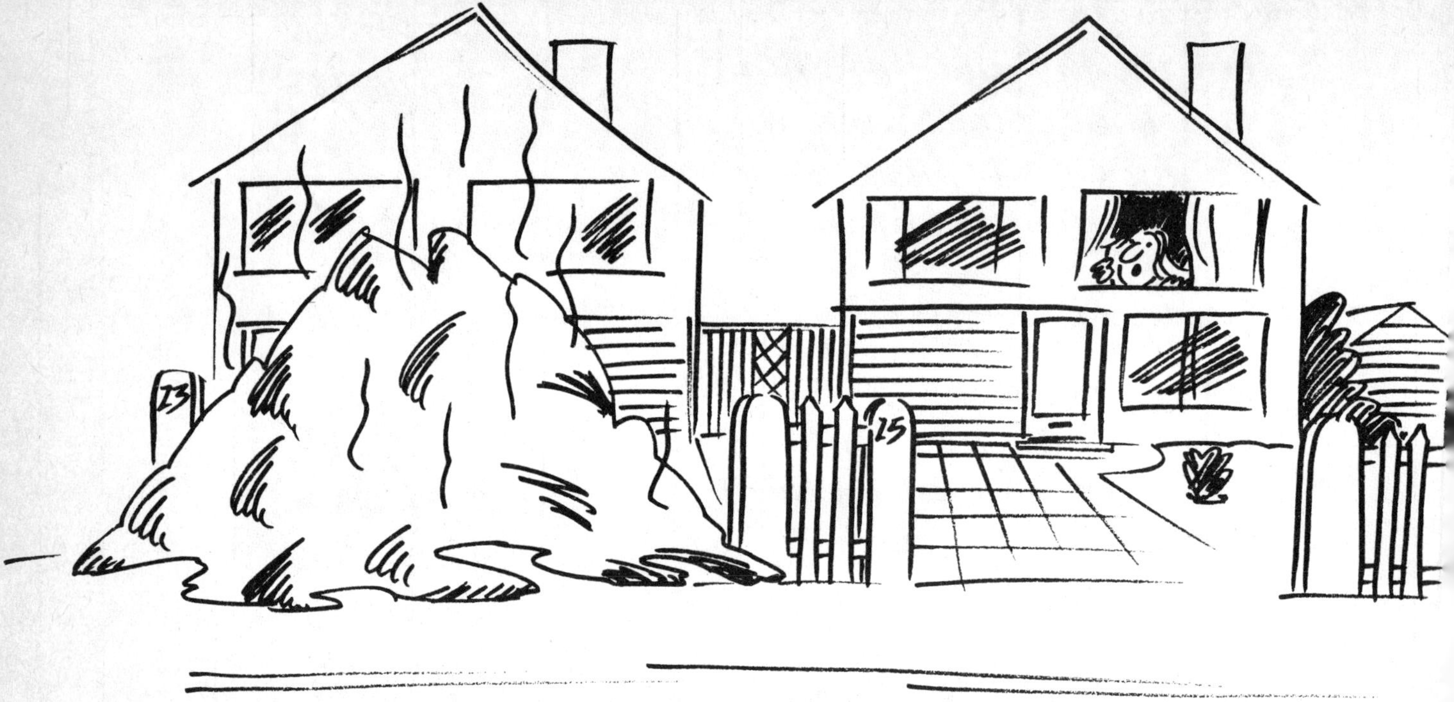
13
15

"Wake up Ted, they've delivered it next door!"

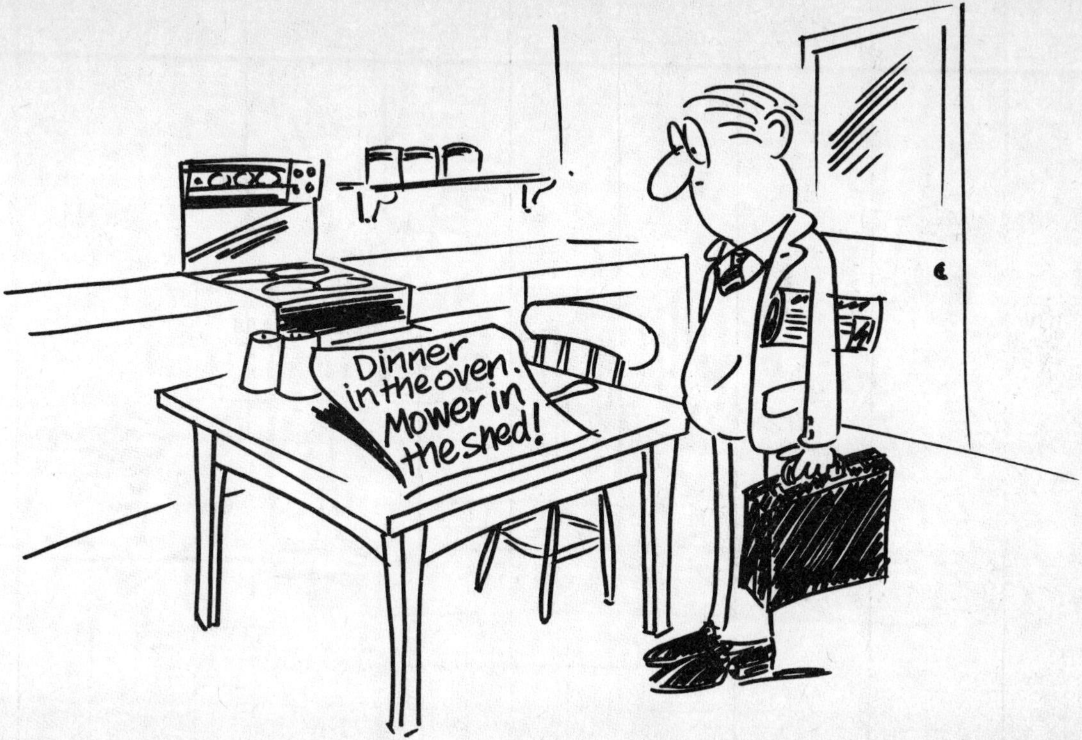
Dinner in the oven. Mower in the shed!

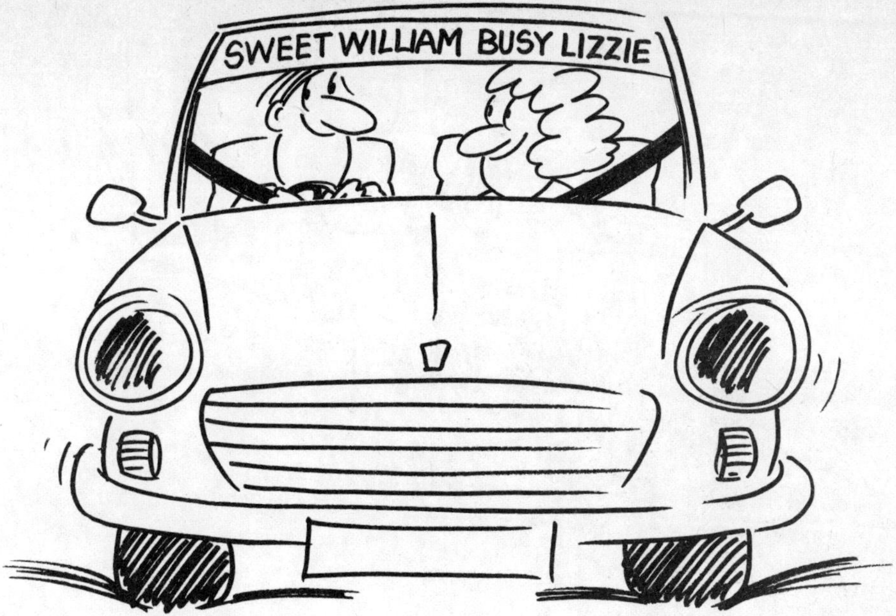
SWEET WILLIAM BUSY LIZZIE

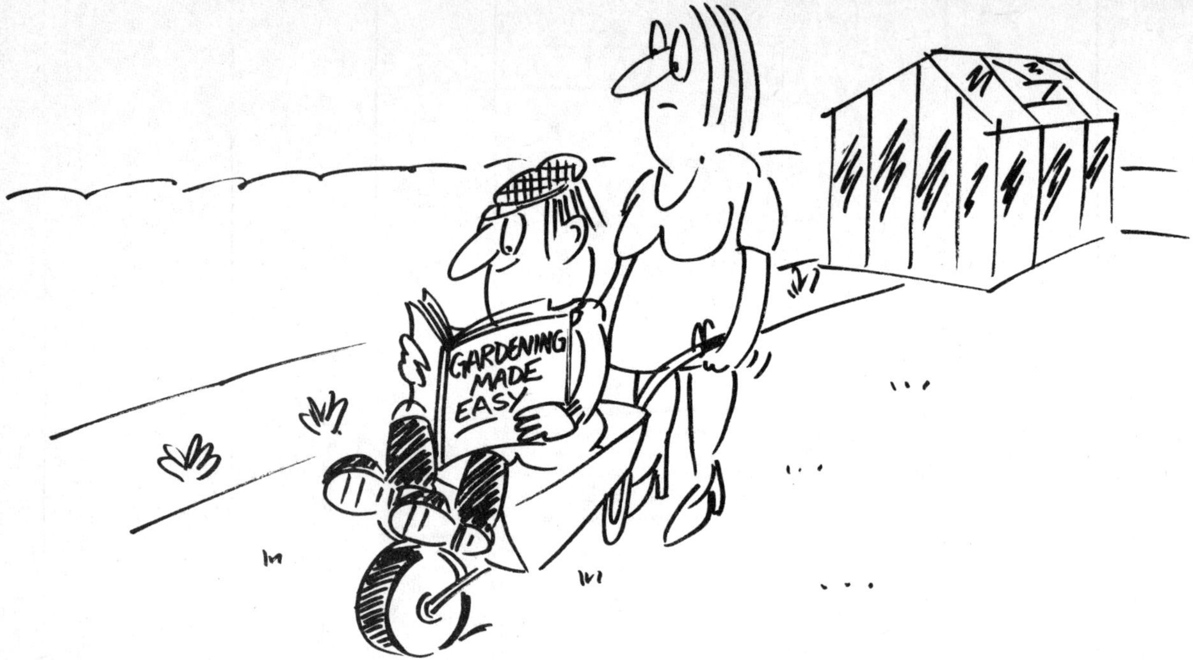
GARDENING
MADE
EASY

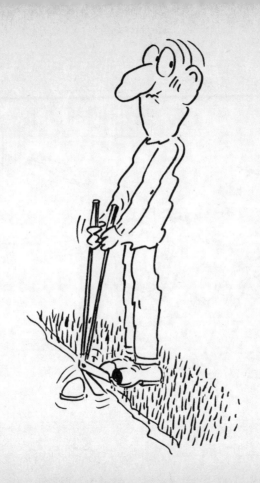

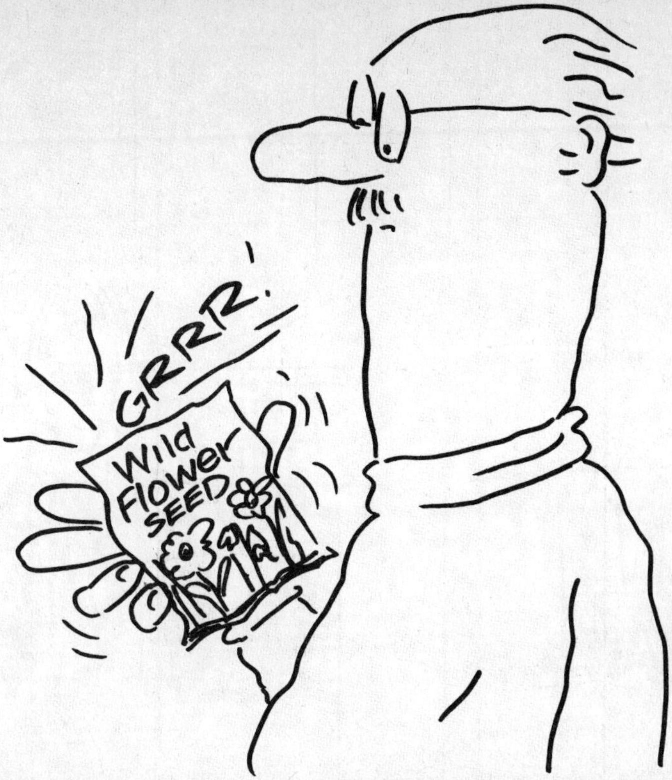
GRRR.
Wild Flower SEED

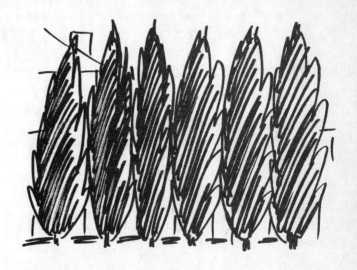

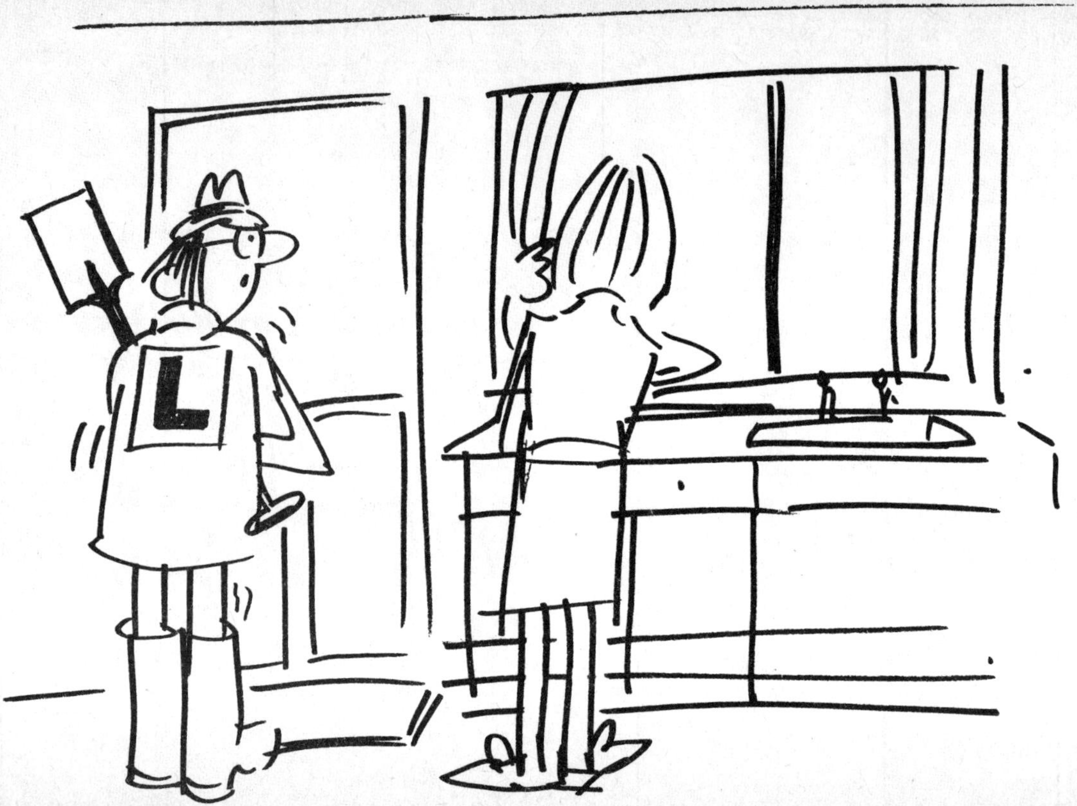
L

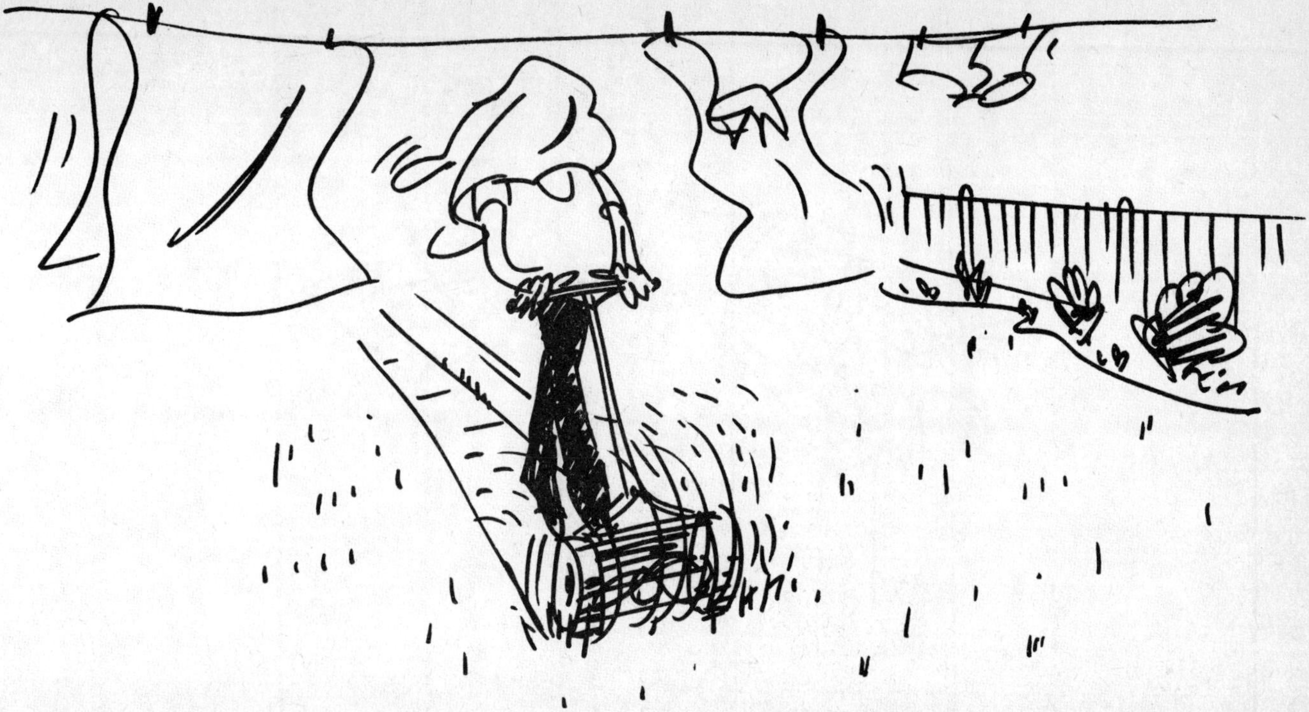

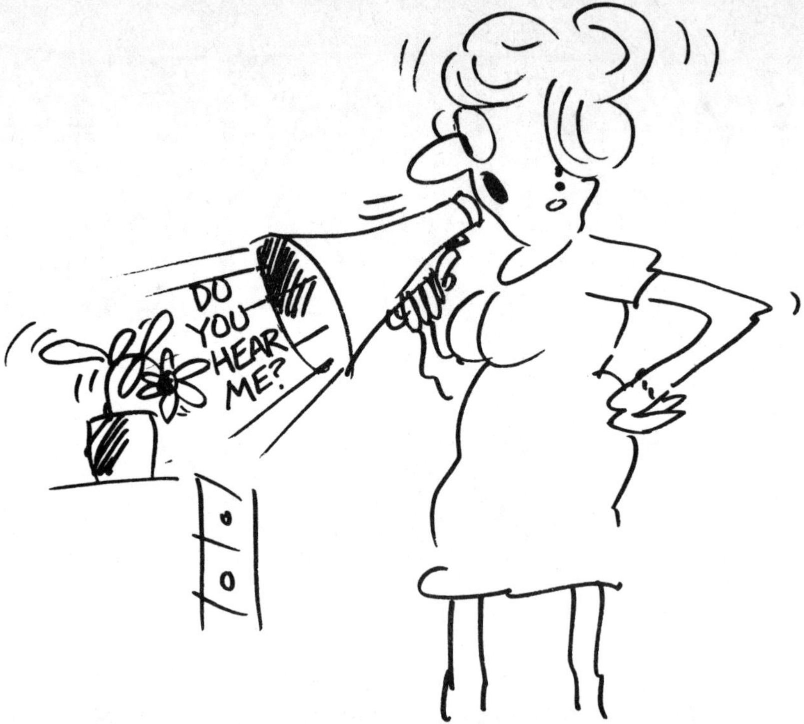
DO YOU HEAR ME?

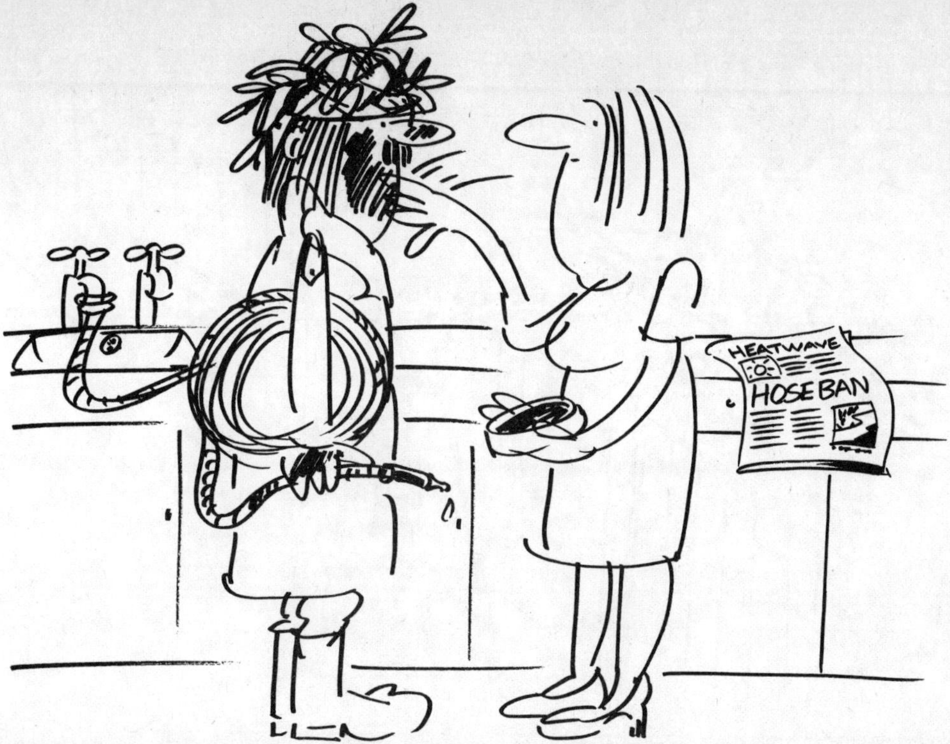
HEATWAVE
HOSE BAN

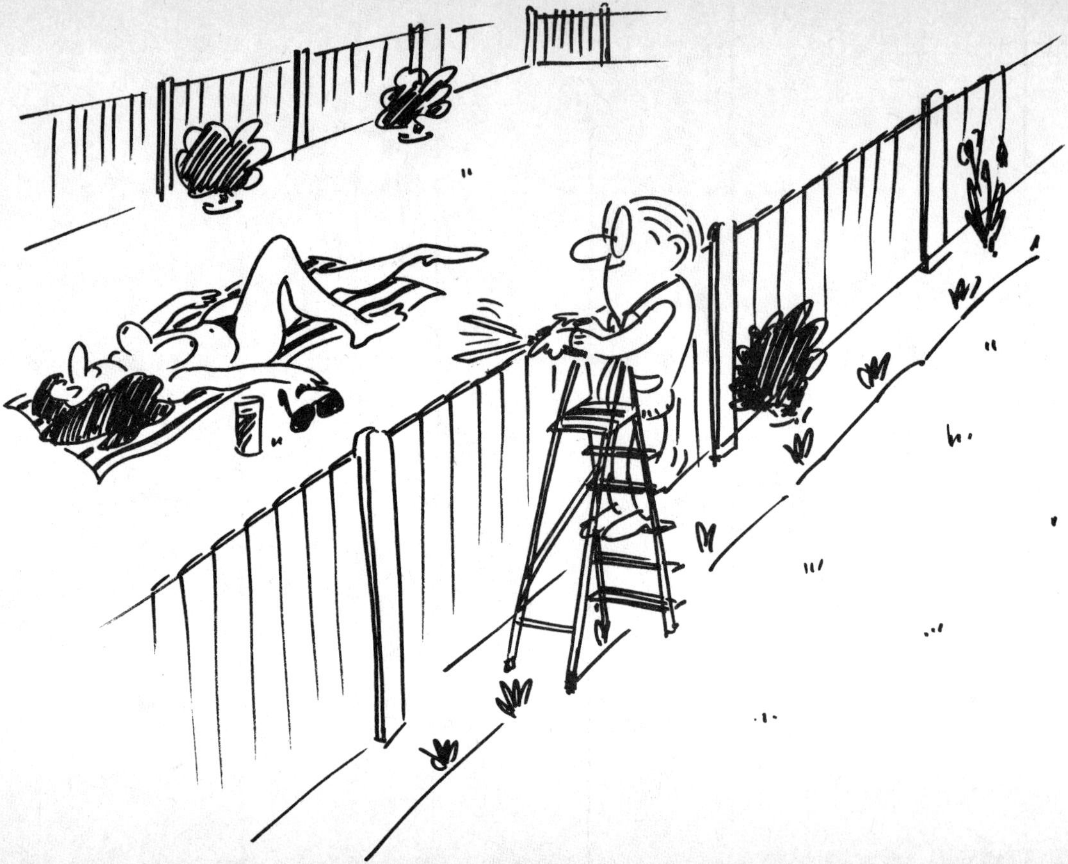

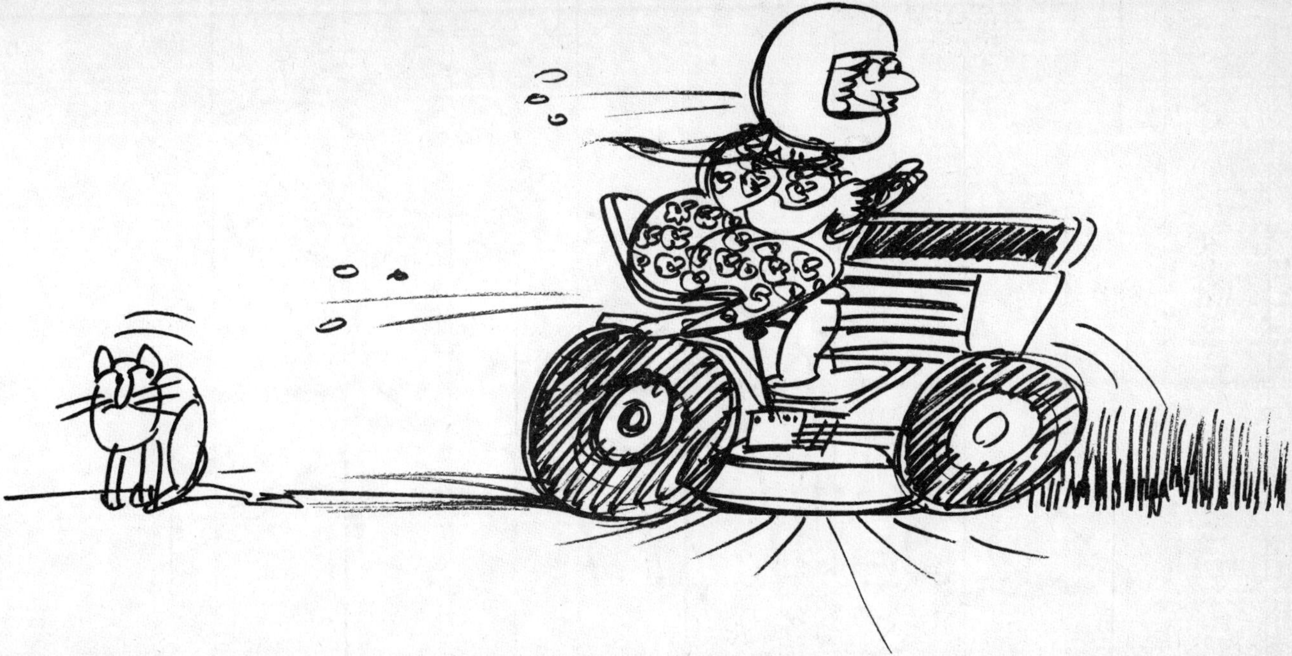

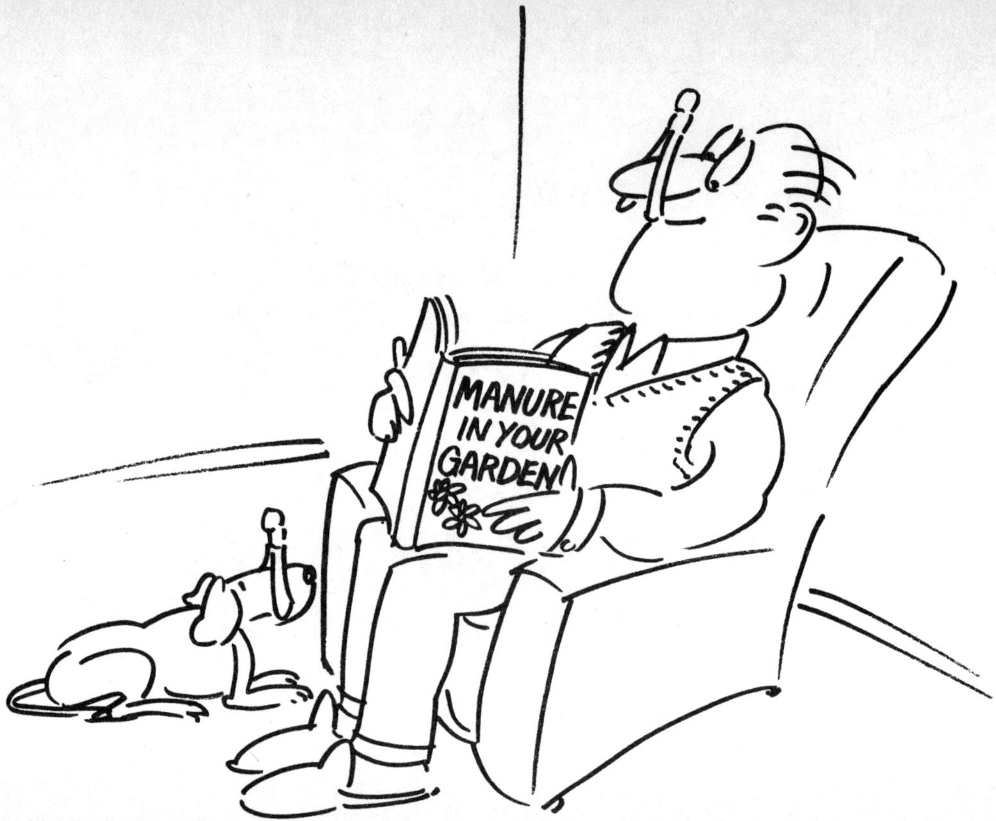
MANURE IN YOUR GARDEN

"There's a weed on the drive!"

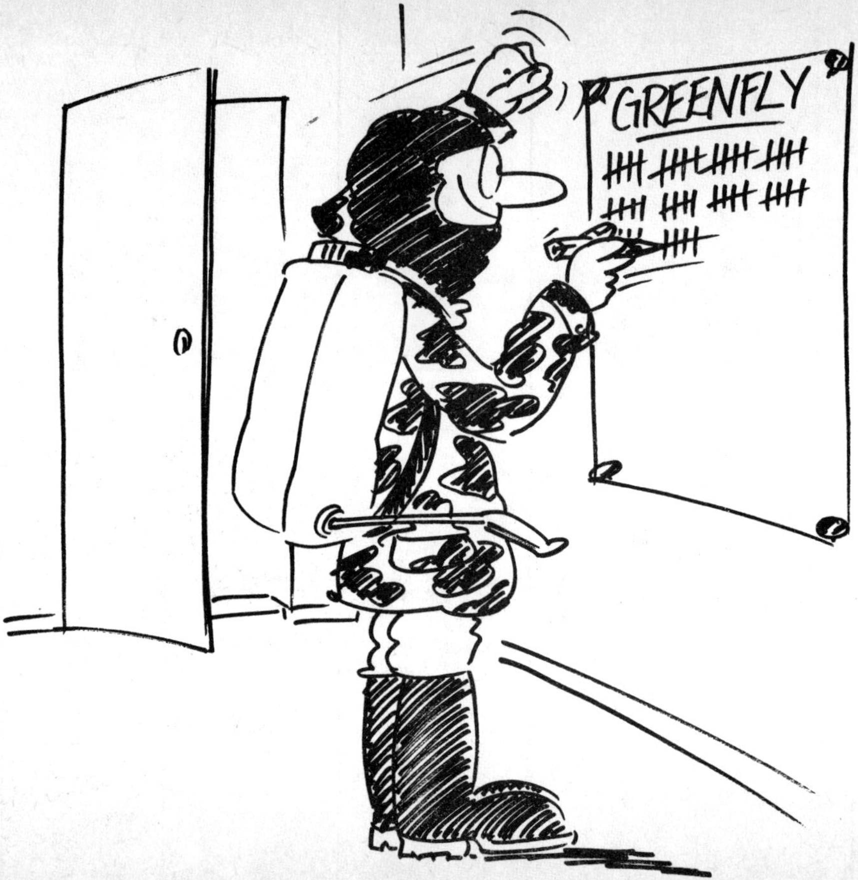
GREENFLY

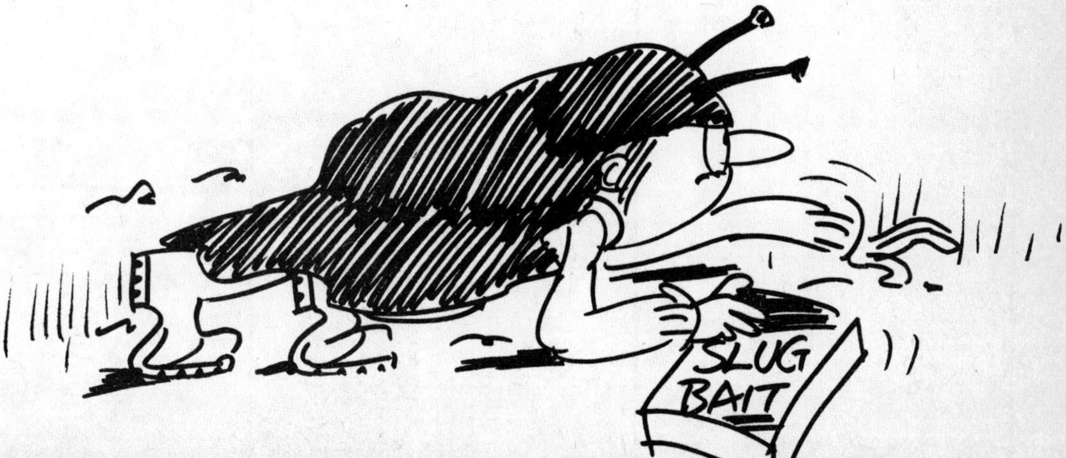
SLUG
BAIT

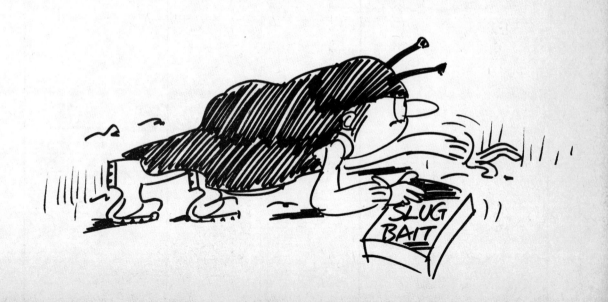

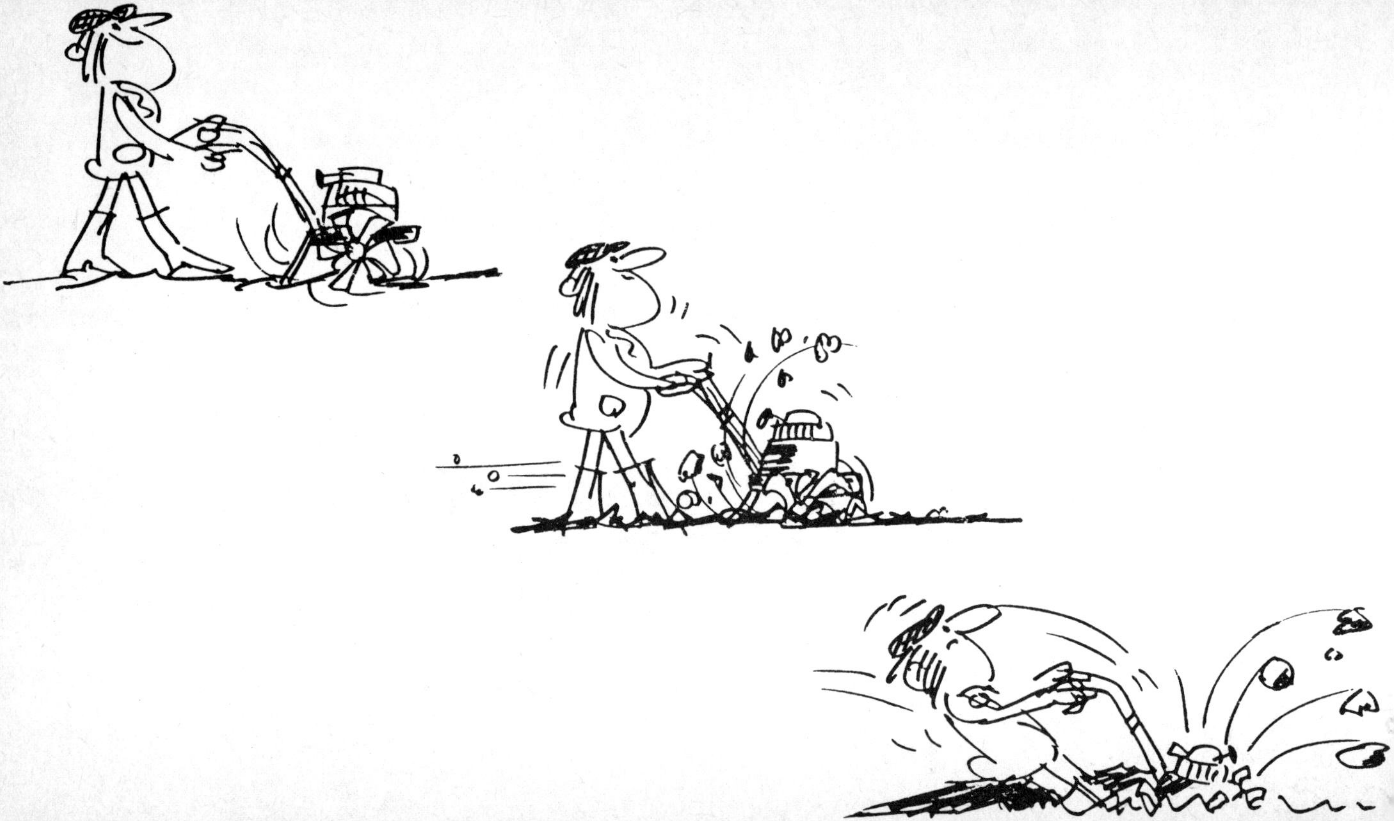

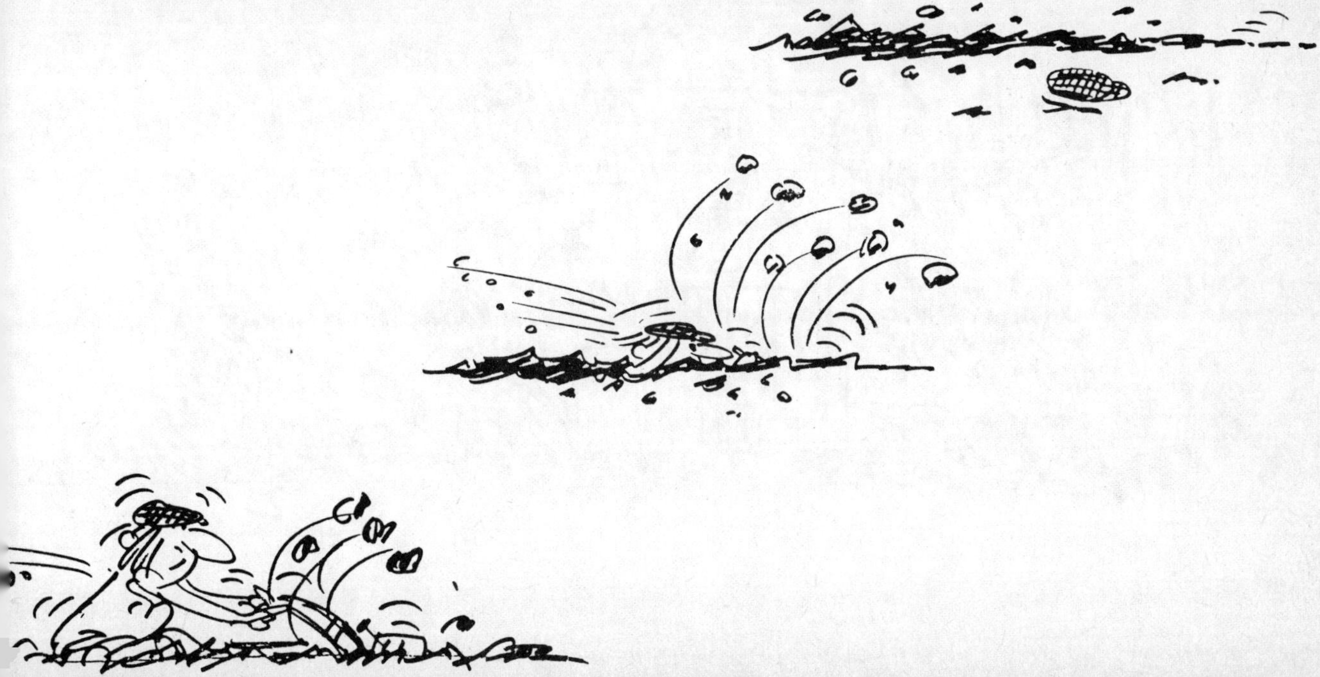

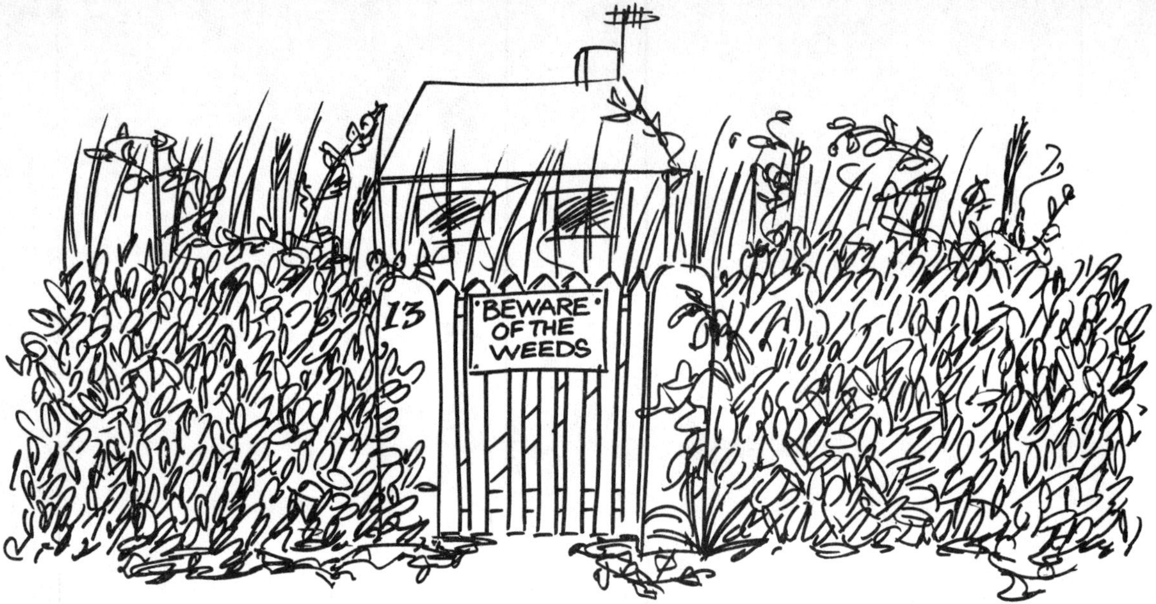
13
BEWARE
OF THE
WEEDS

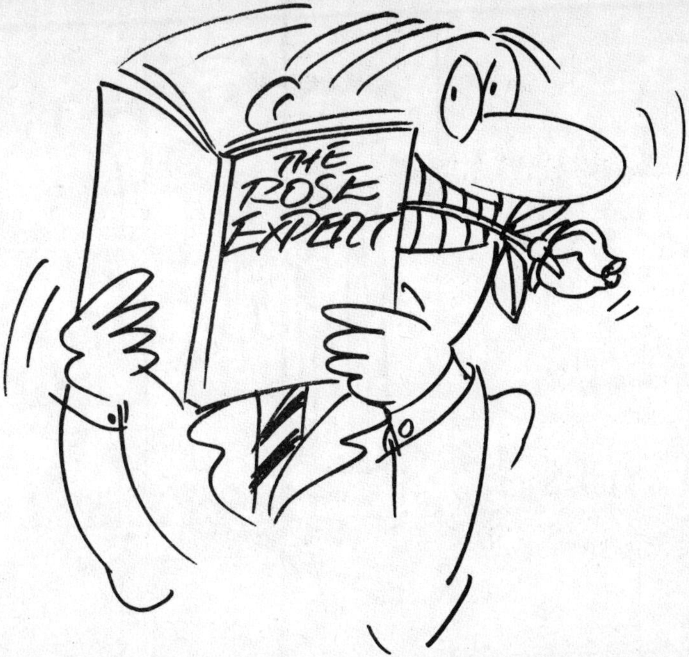
THE ROSE EXPERT

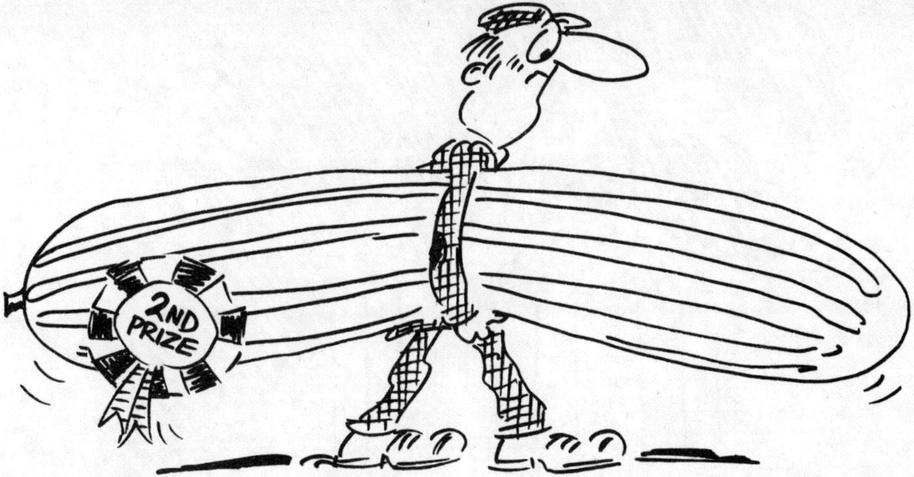
2ND
PRIZE

"It is Sunday you know!"

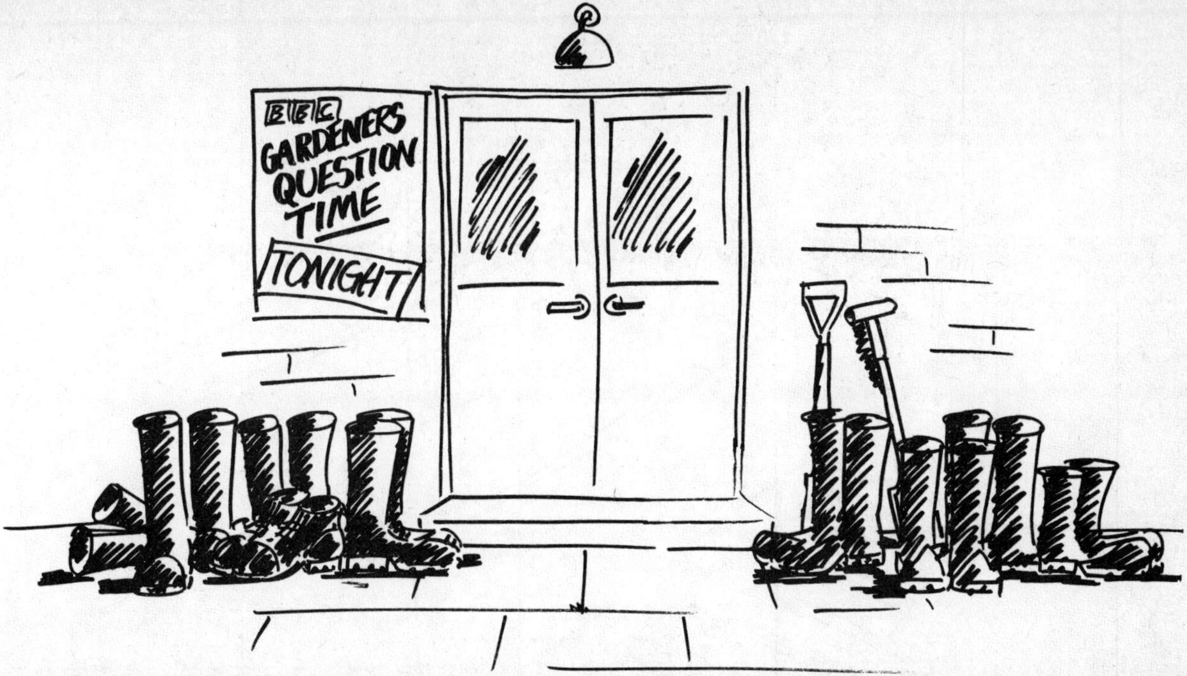
BBC
GARDENERS QUESTION TIME
TONIGHT

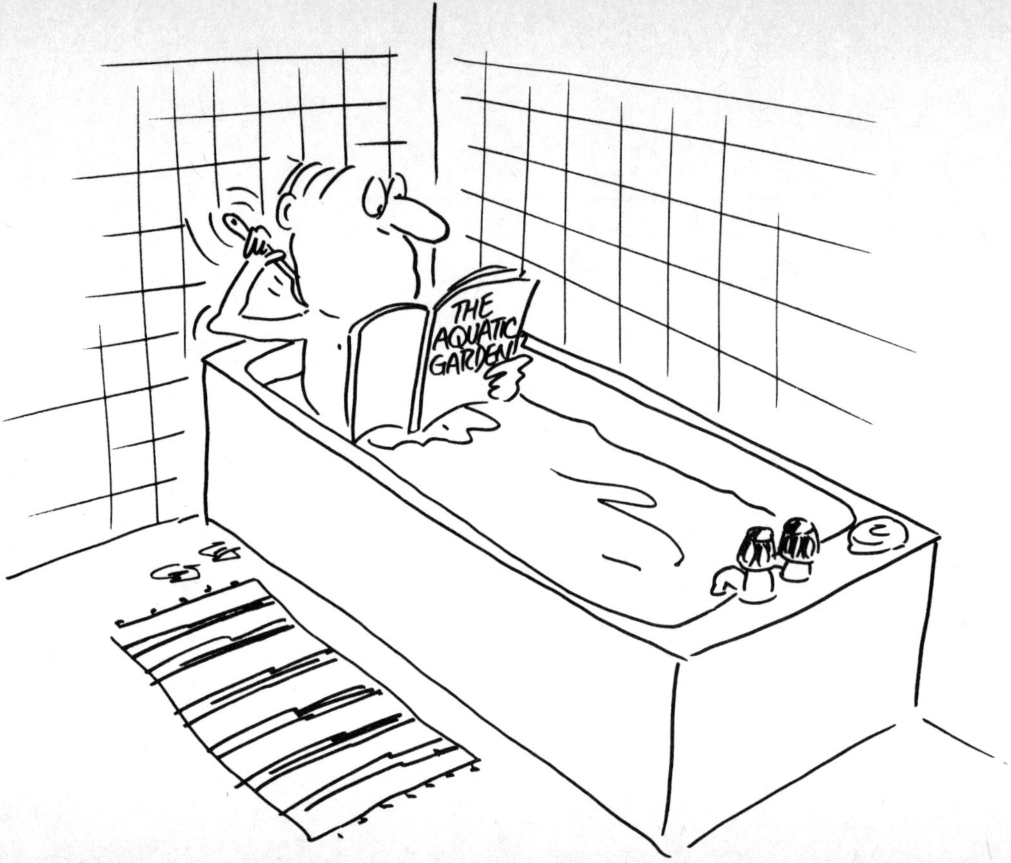
THE AQUATIC GARDEN

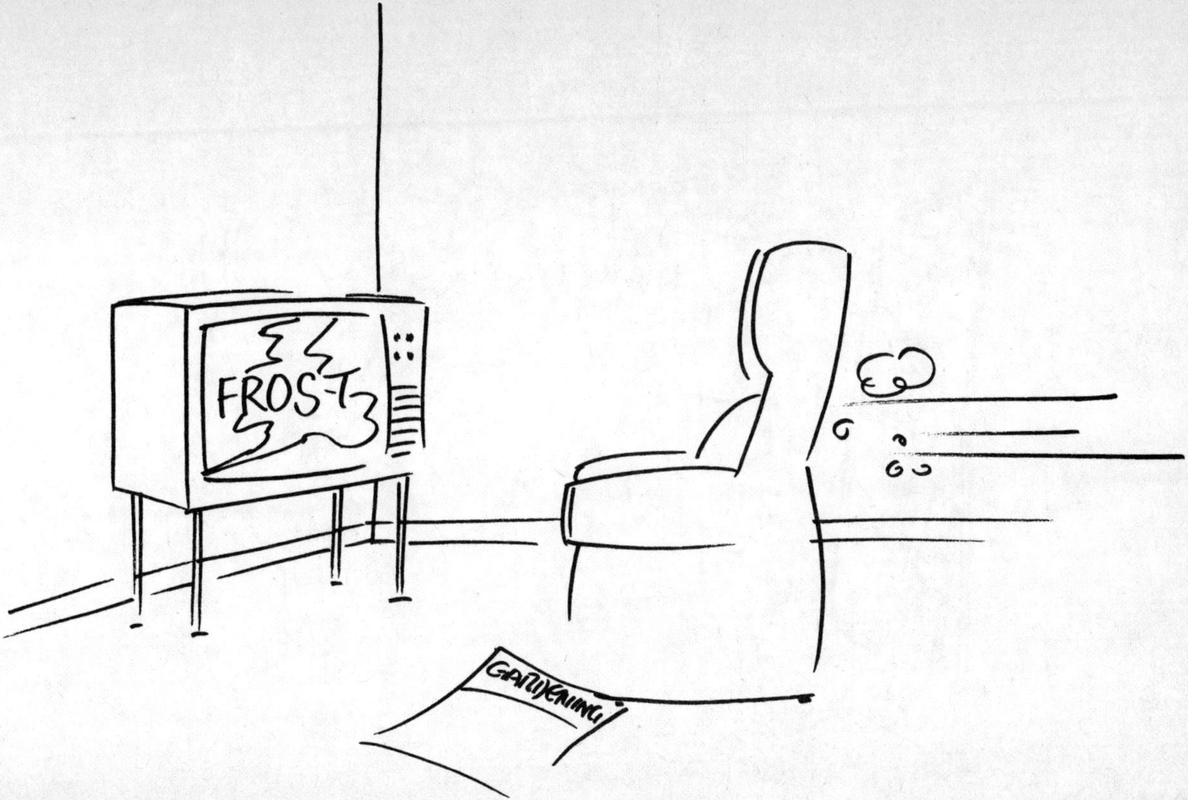
FROS-T
GARDENING

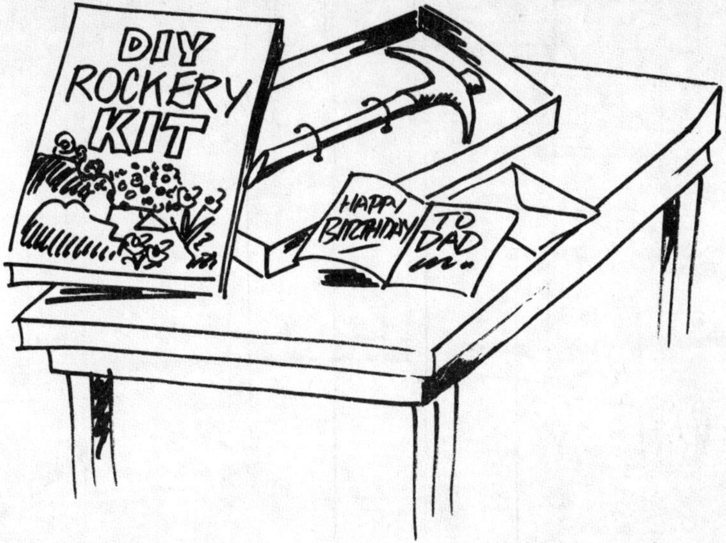
DIY
ROCKERY
KIT
HAPPY
BIRTHDAY
TO
DAD

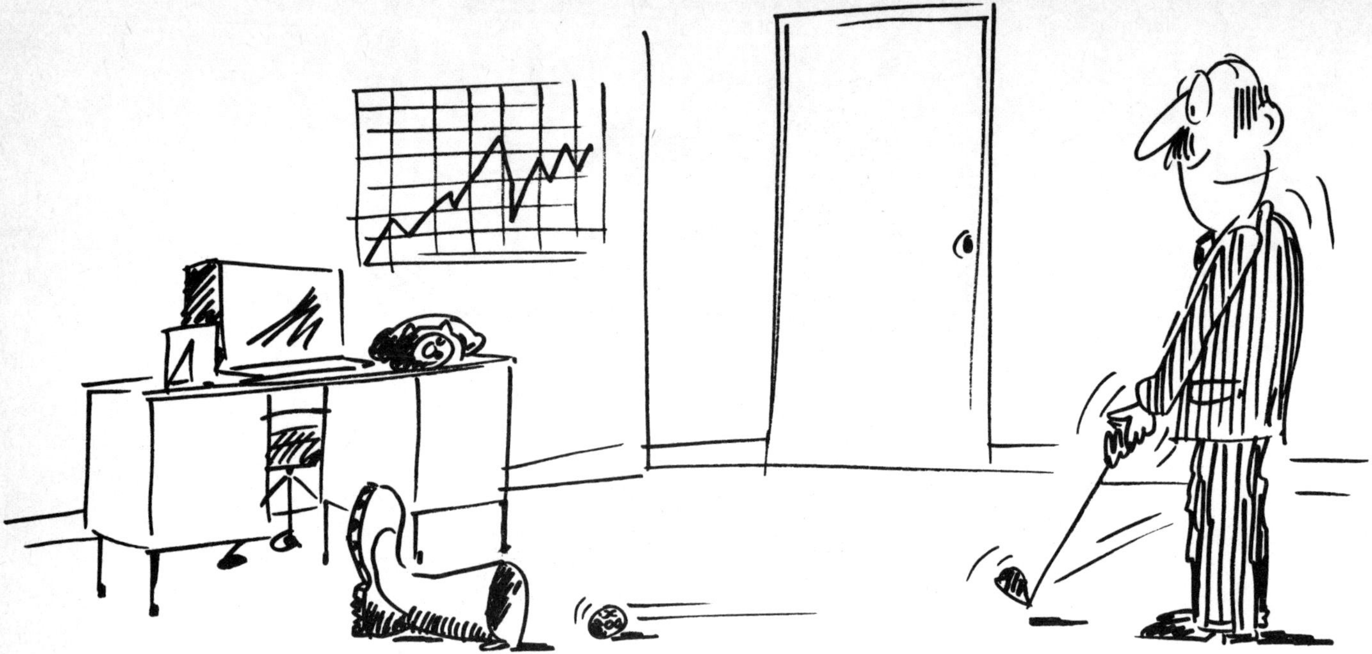

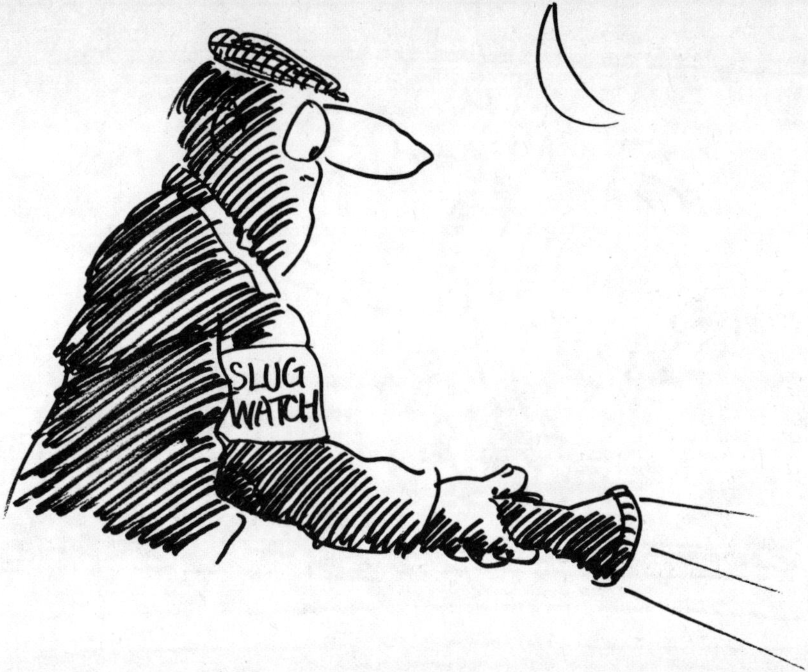
SLUG
WATCH

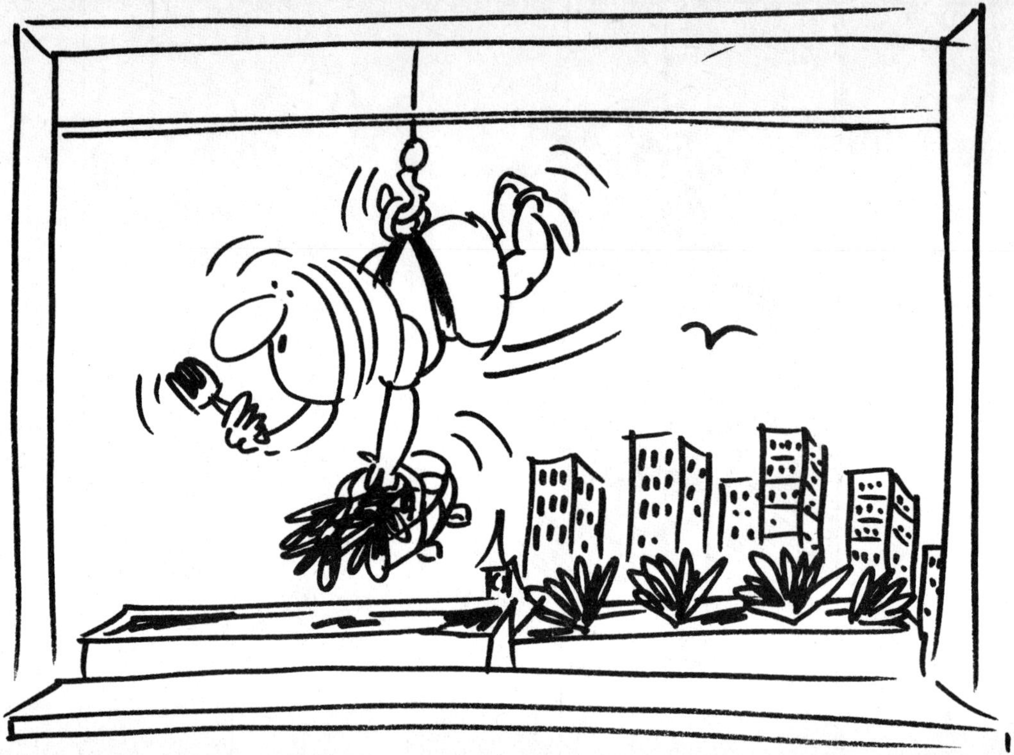

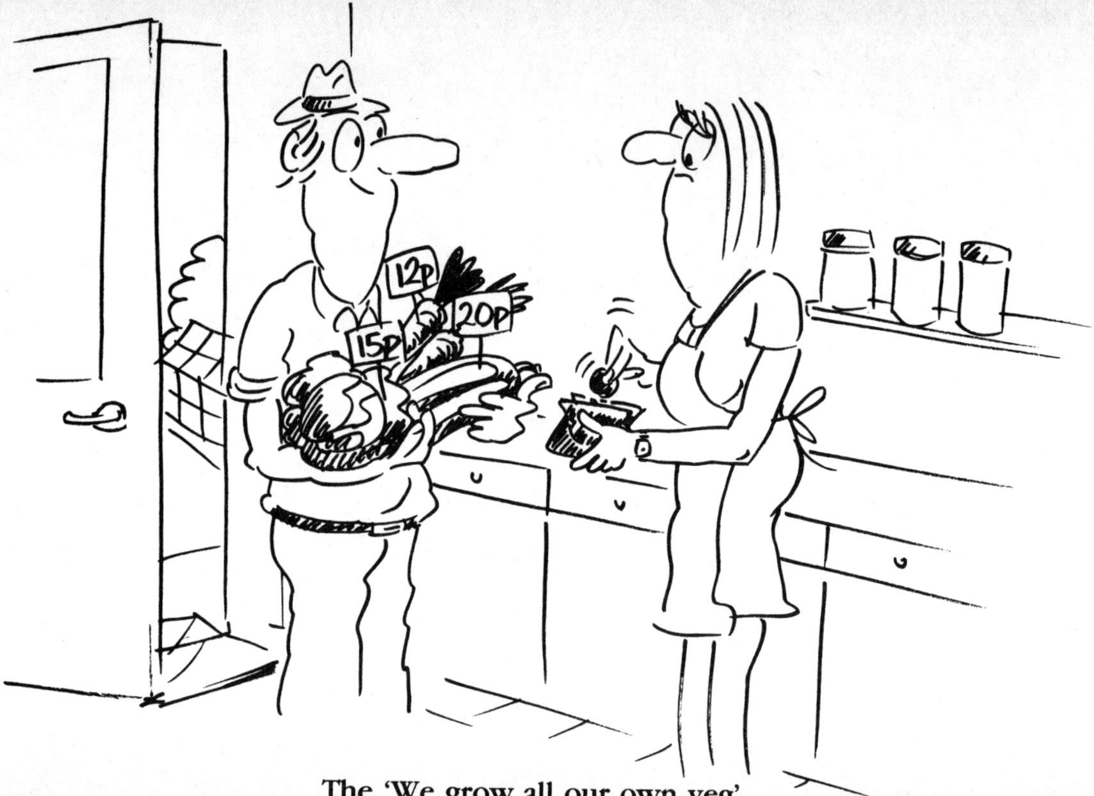
12p
20p
15p

The 'We grow all our own veg'
Gardeners

The Town Gardener

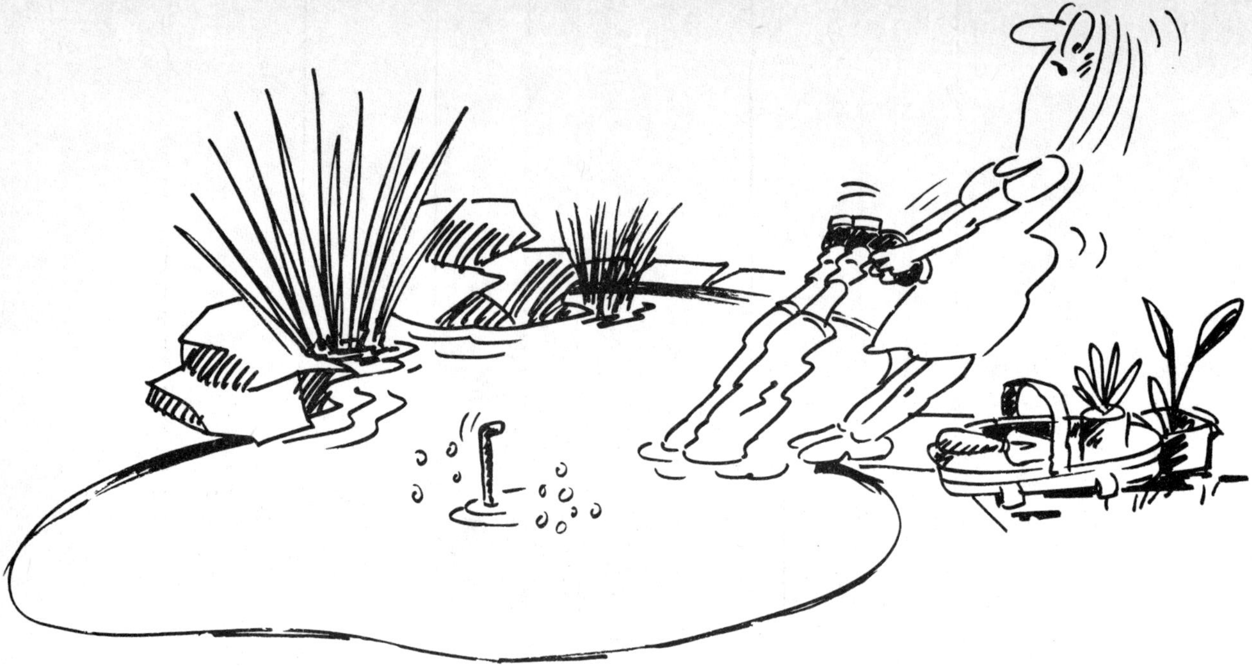

The Aquatic Gardener

The 'My Runners are this high'
Gardener

The Cottage Gardener

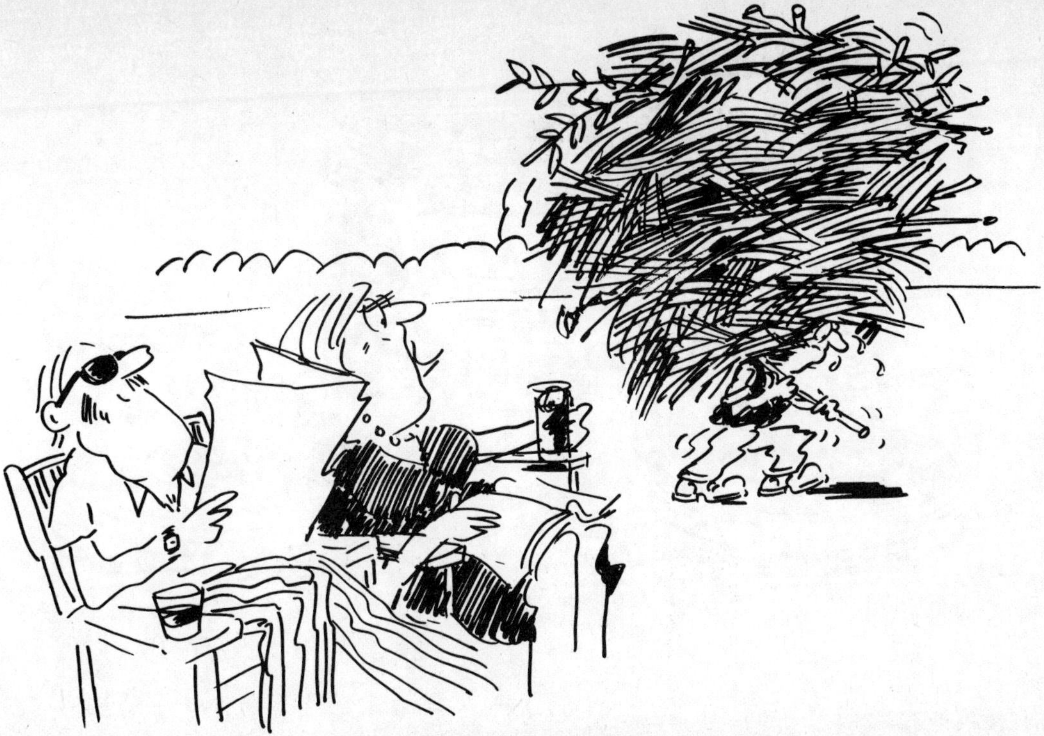

The 'We've got a little man
who helps us' Gardeners

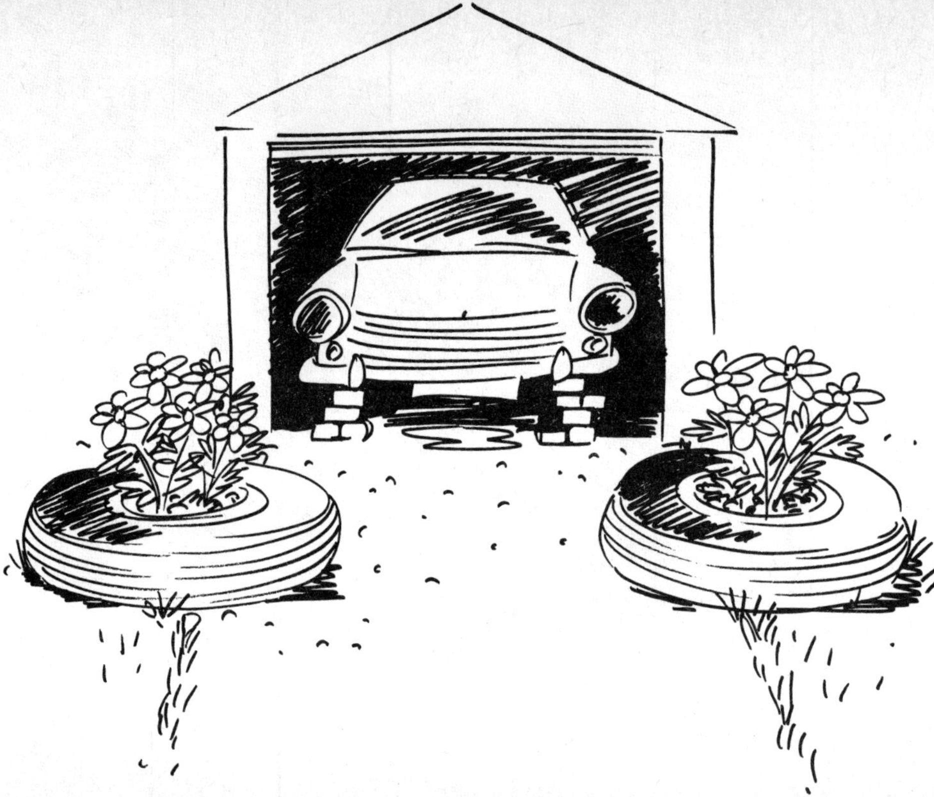

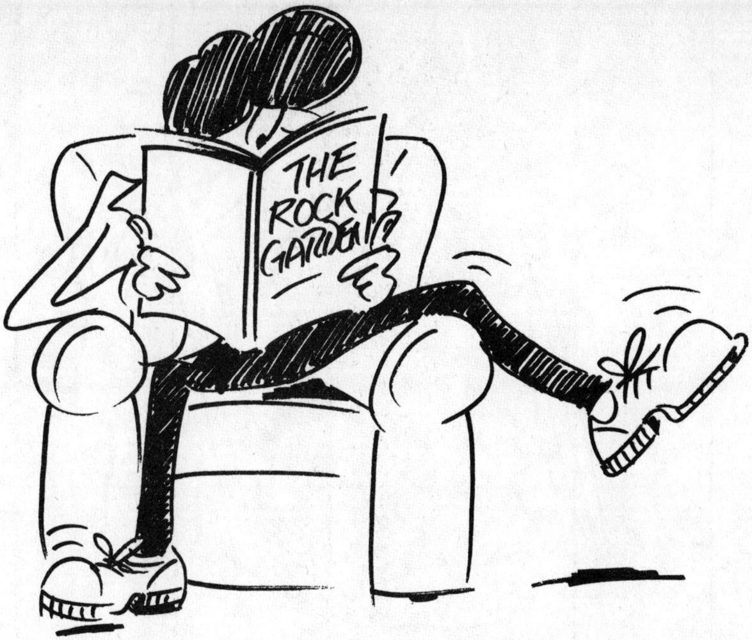
THE ROCK GARDEN

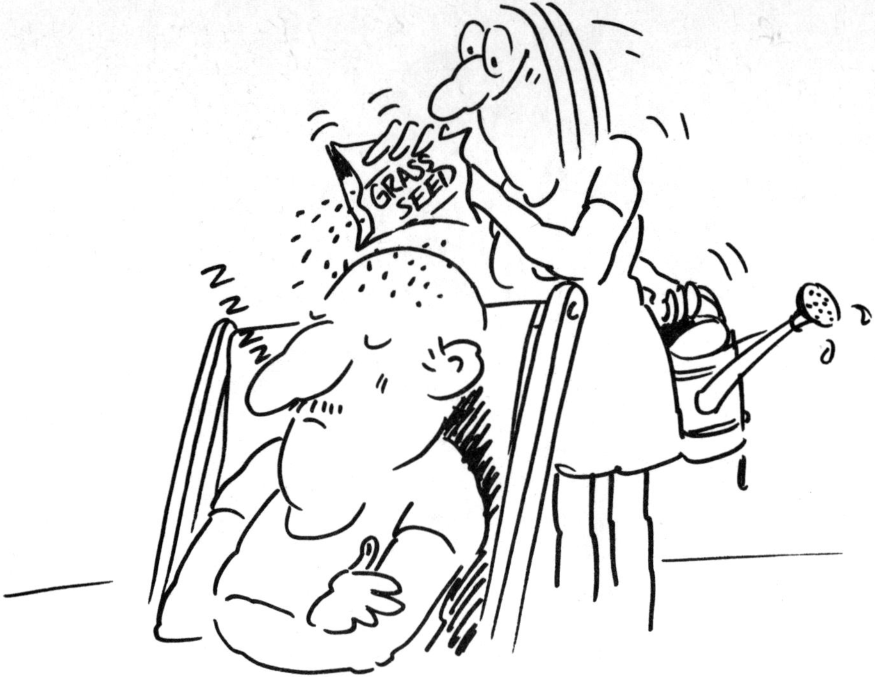
GRASS SEED
ZZZ
ZZZ

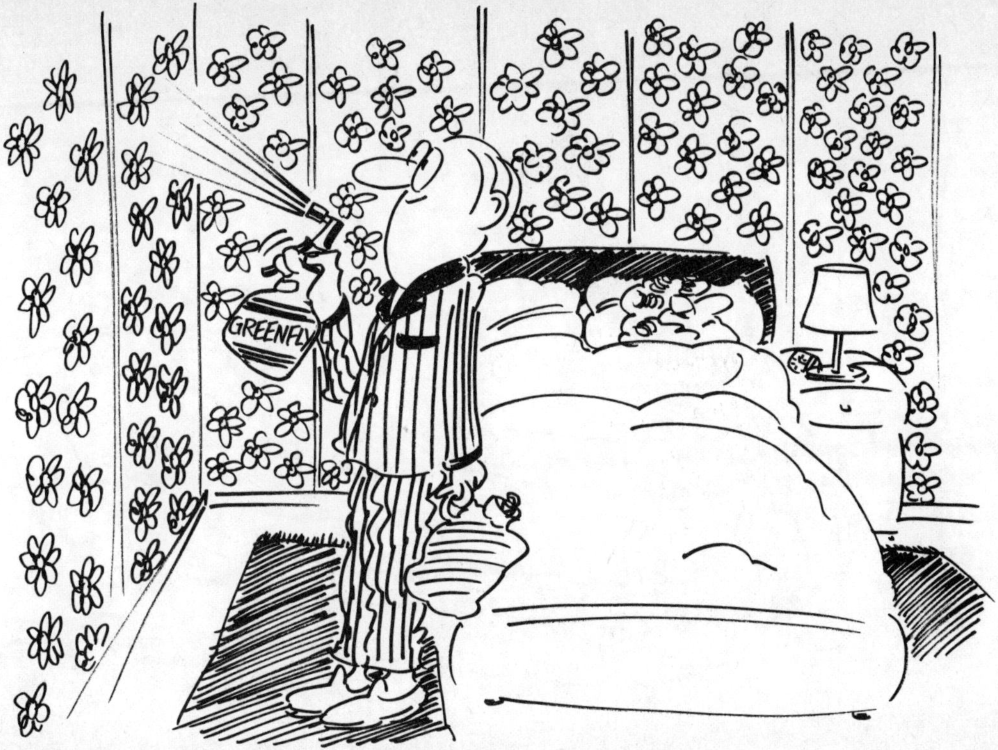
GREENFLY

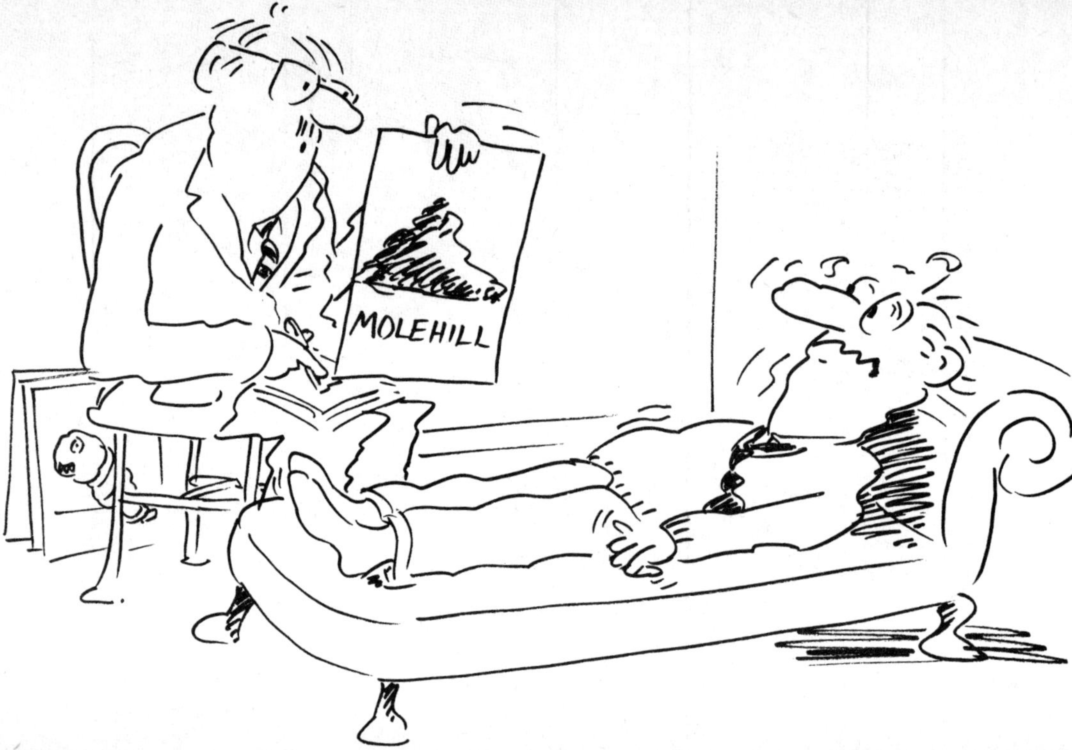
MOLEHILL

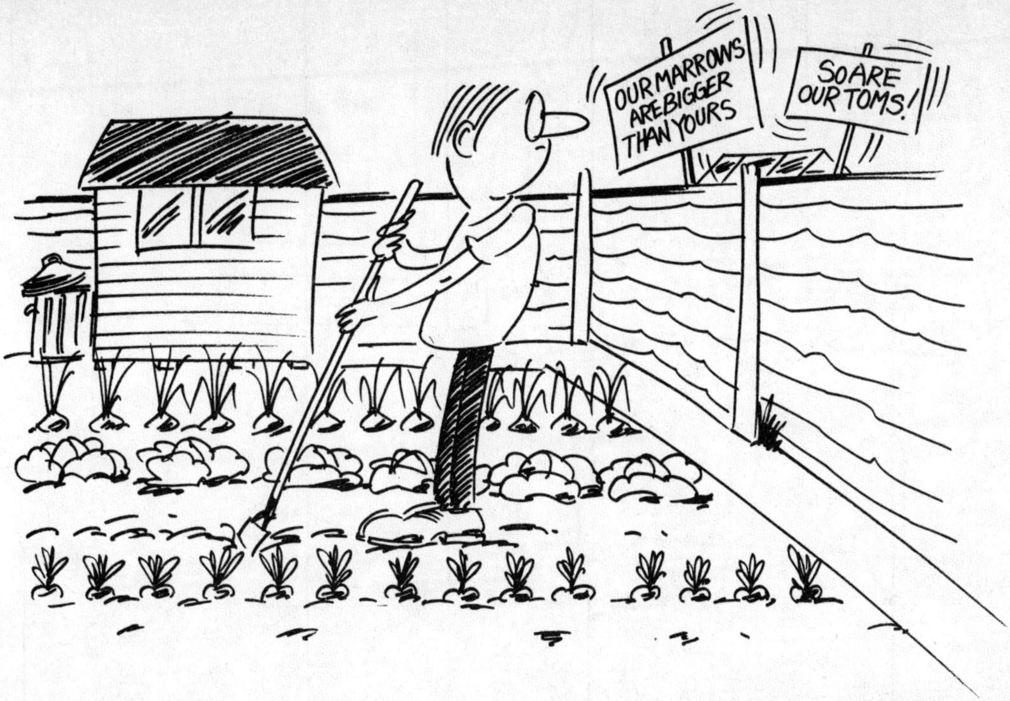
OUR MARROWS ARE BIGGER THAN YOURS
SO ARE OUR TOMS!

"... and take your boots off
before you come in!"

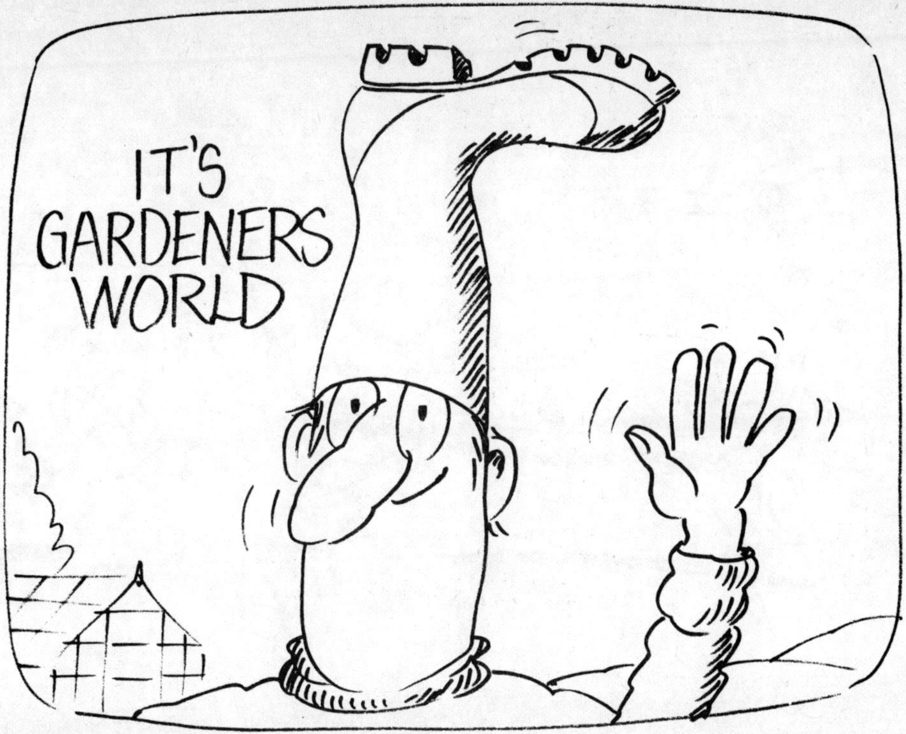
IT'S
GARDENERS
WORLD

TREE
SURGEON

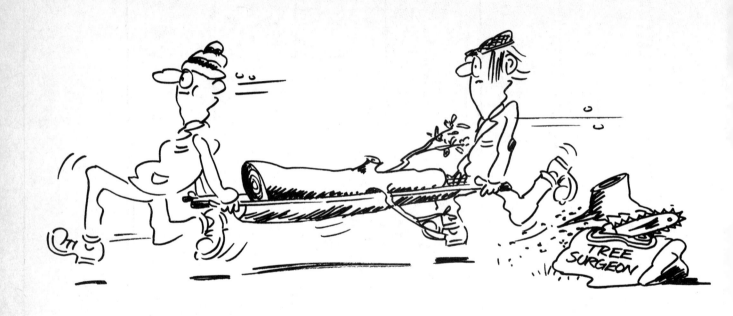

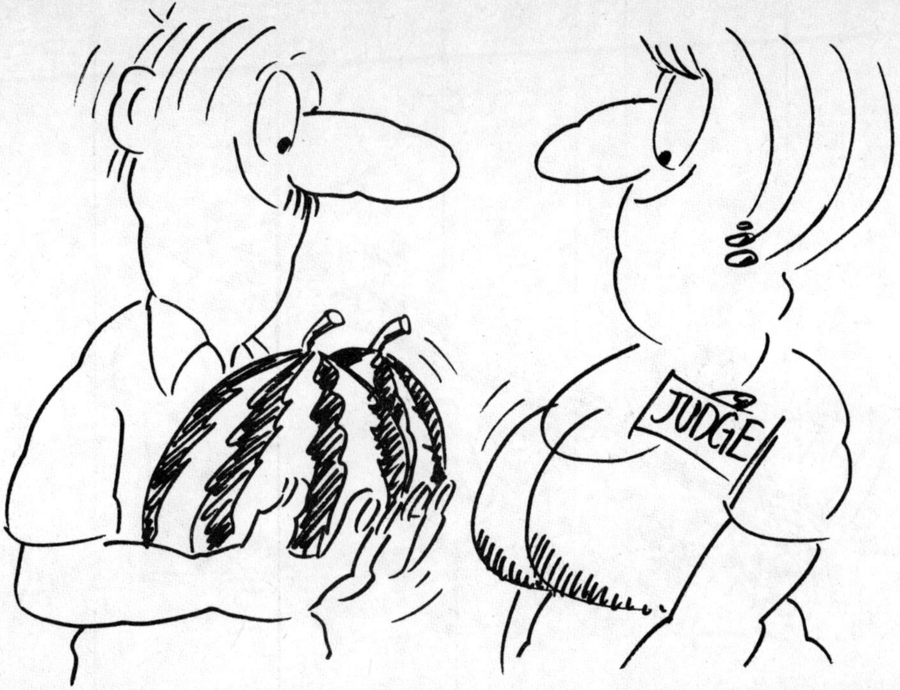
JUDGE

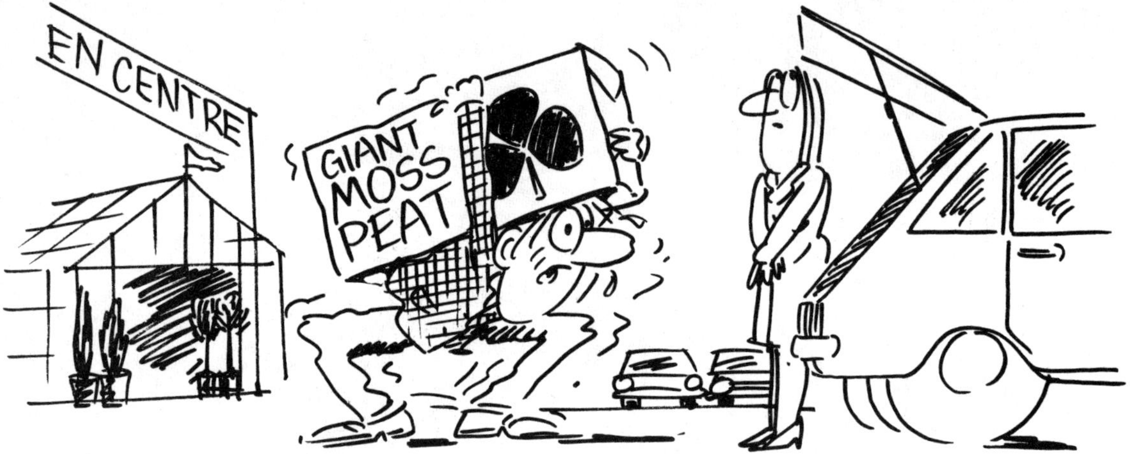
EN CENTRE
GIANT MOSS PEAT

GARDENING?
FOR THE MAN WHO DOESN'T WANT TO!
Avoid the nagging and backache any weekend when you've just had enough
PLASTER CAST EXCUSE
JUST SLIP IT ON!
GUARANTEED TO DECEIVE!
Delivered in plain wrapper
SEND NOW

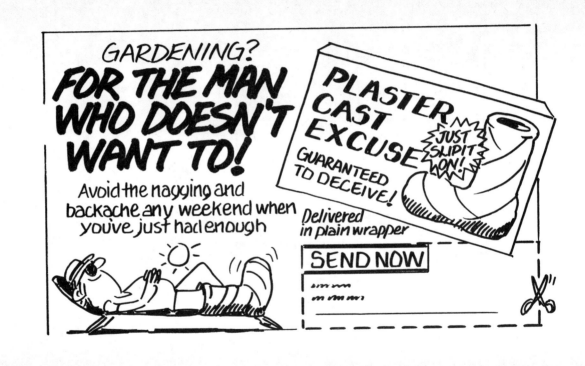

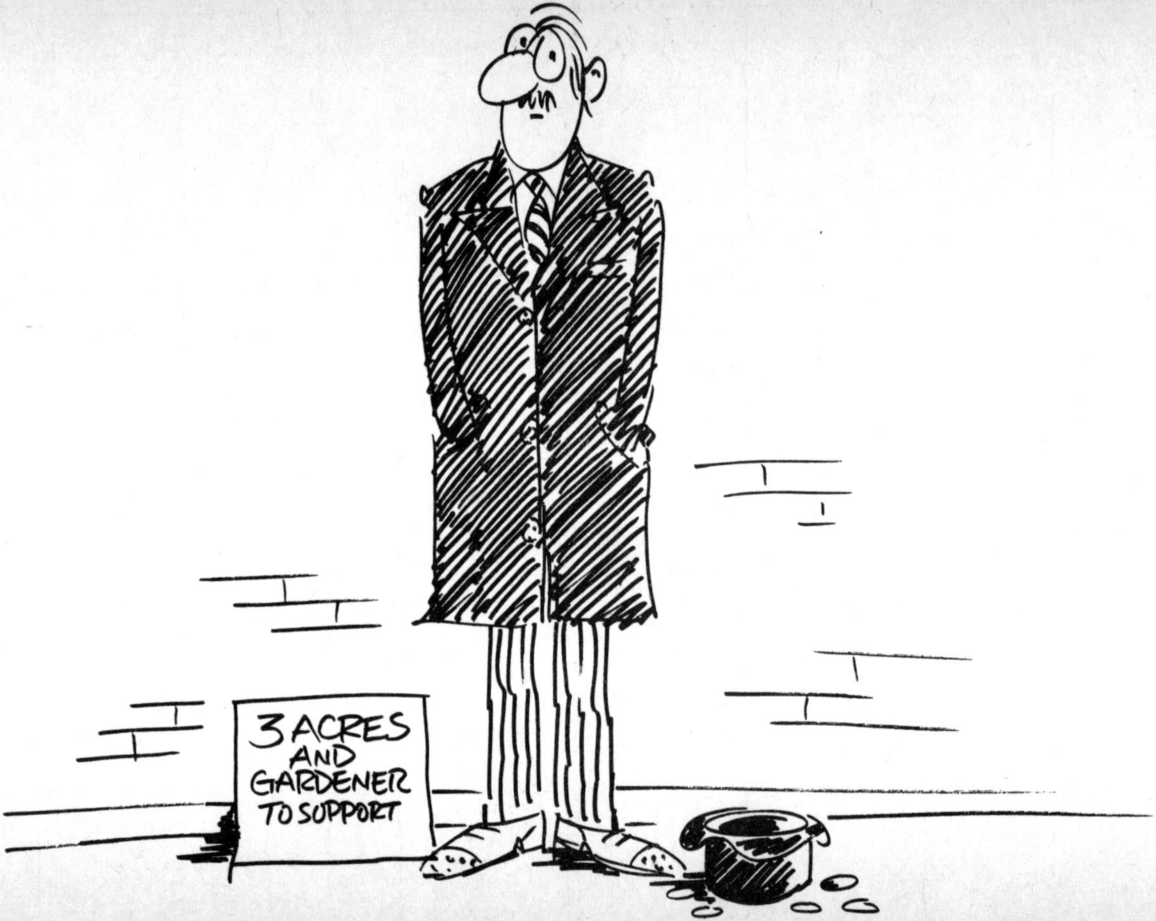
3 ACRES AND GARDENER TO SUPPORT

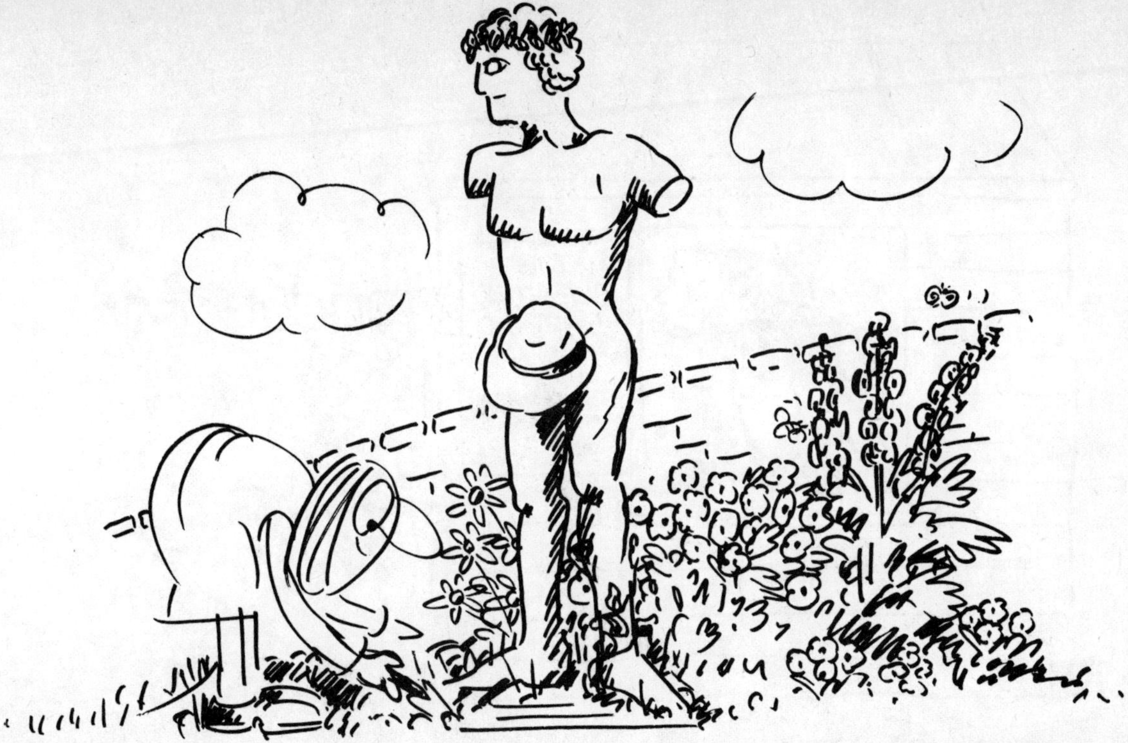

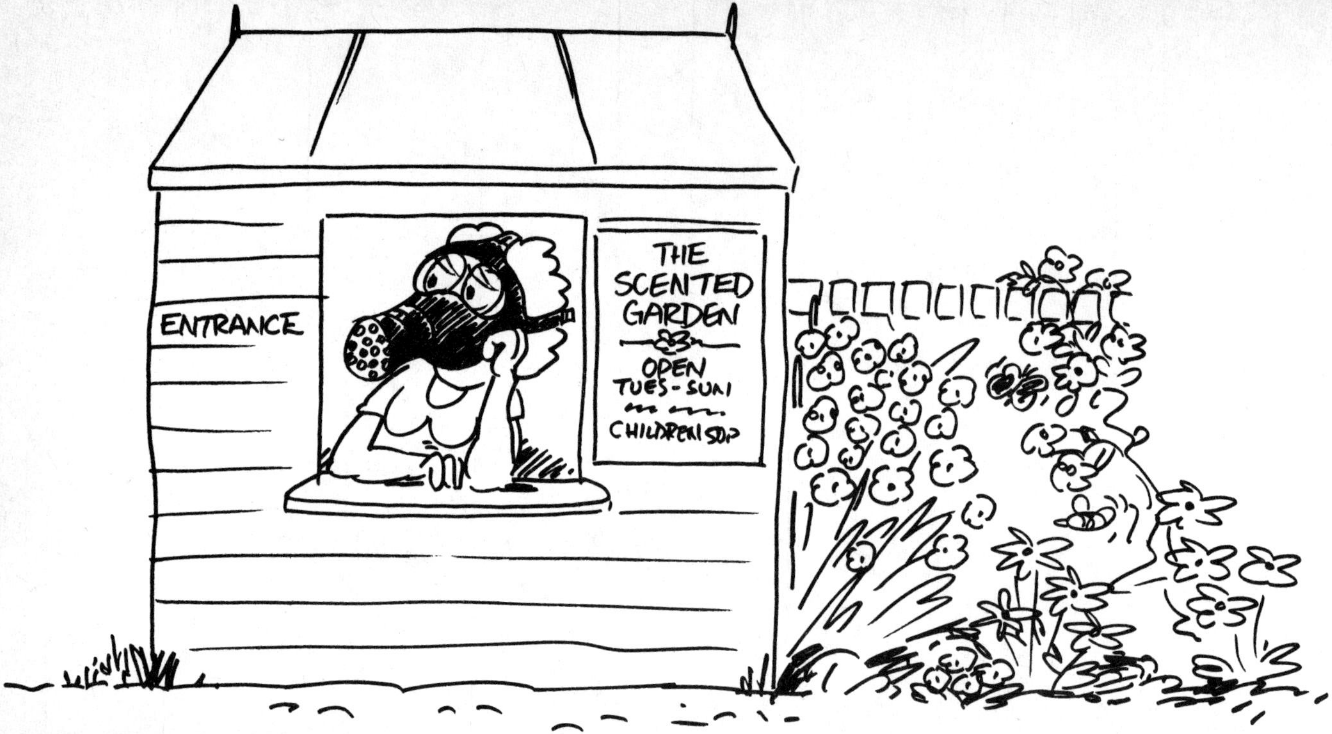
ENTRANCE
THE SCENTED GARDEN
OPEN
TUES - SUN
CHILDREN 50p

STRIMMER
HEDGE CUTTER
MOWER
CHAIN SAW
CULTIVATOR
SHREDDER
GREEN HOUSE
KETTLE

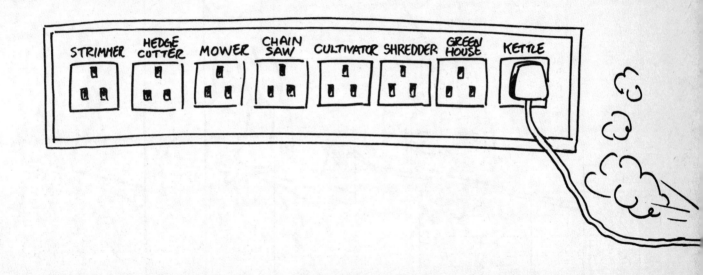

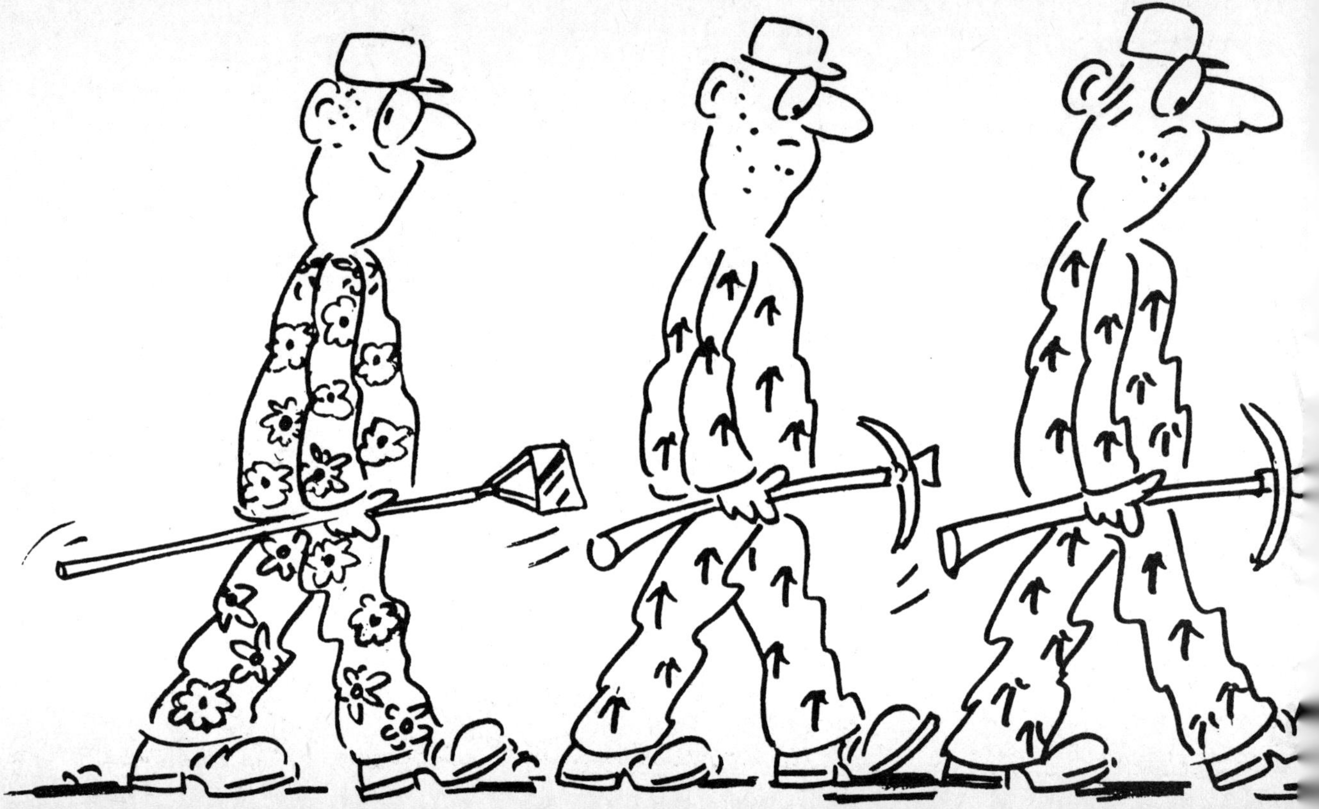

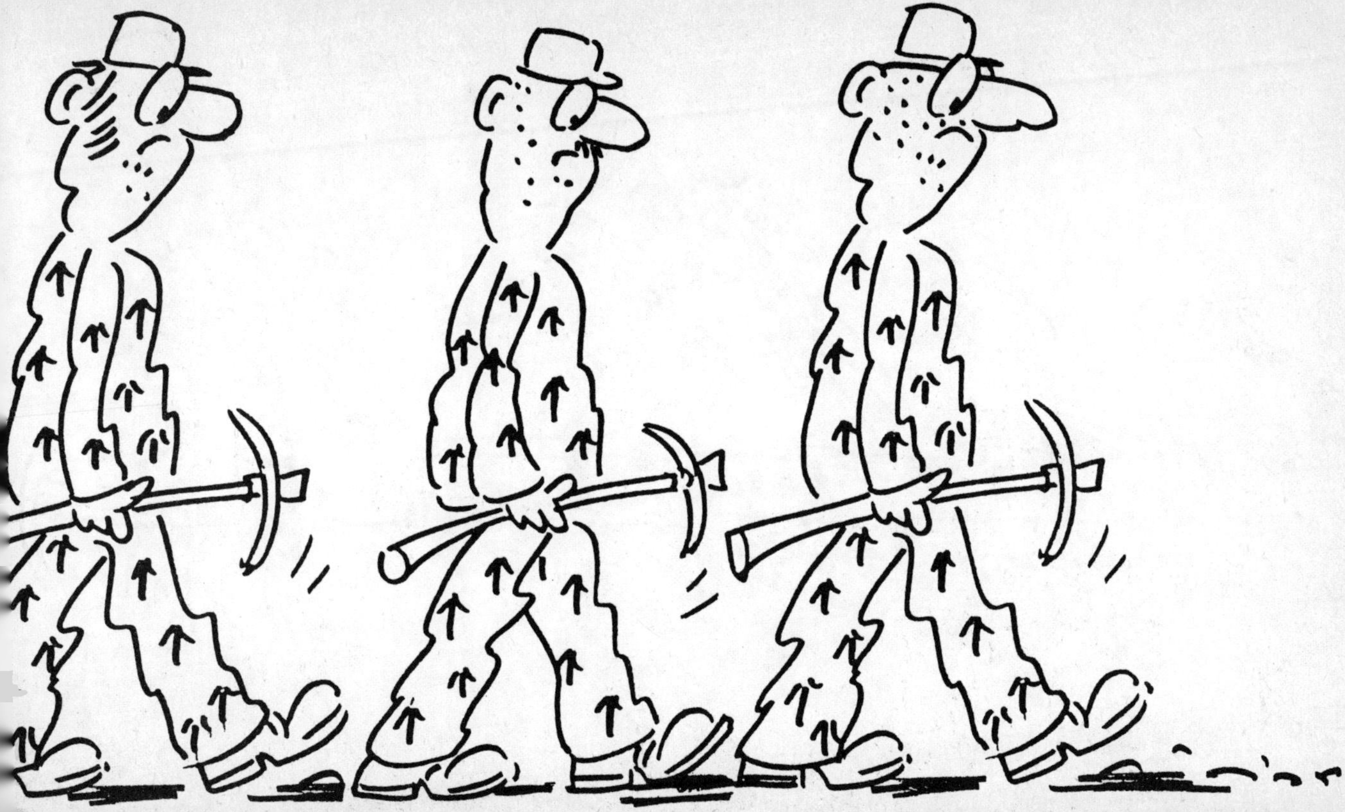

"I'm sure that's deep enough for the runner beans Fred!"

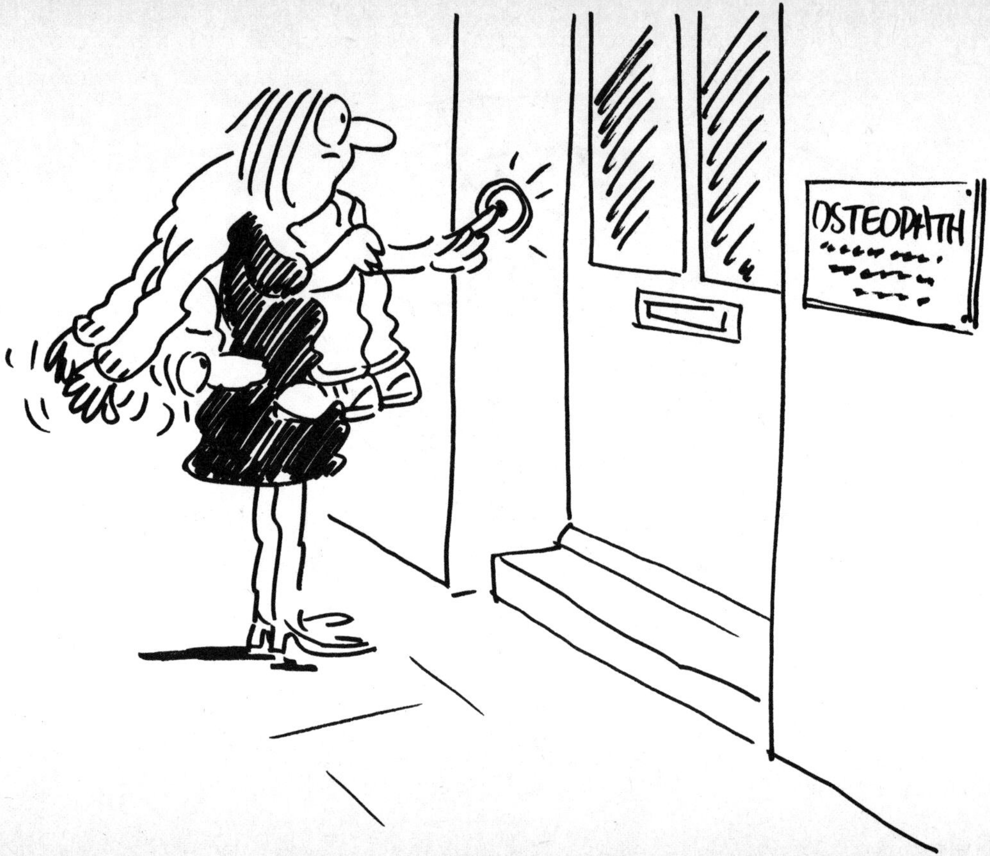
OSTEOPATH

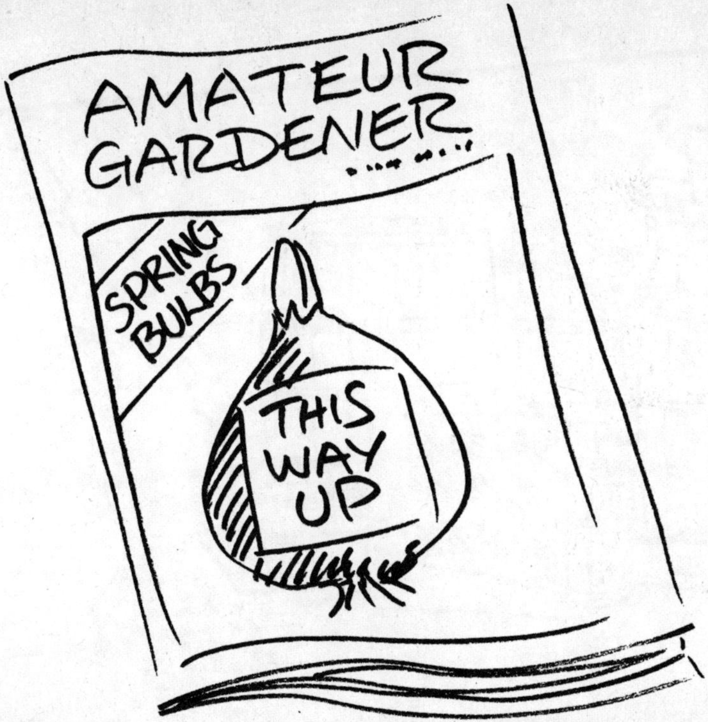
AMATEUR
GARDENER
SPRING
BULBS
THIS
WAY
UP

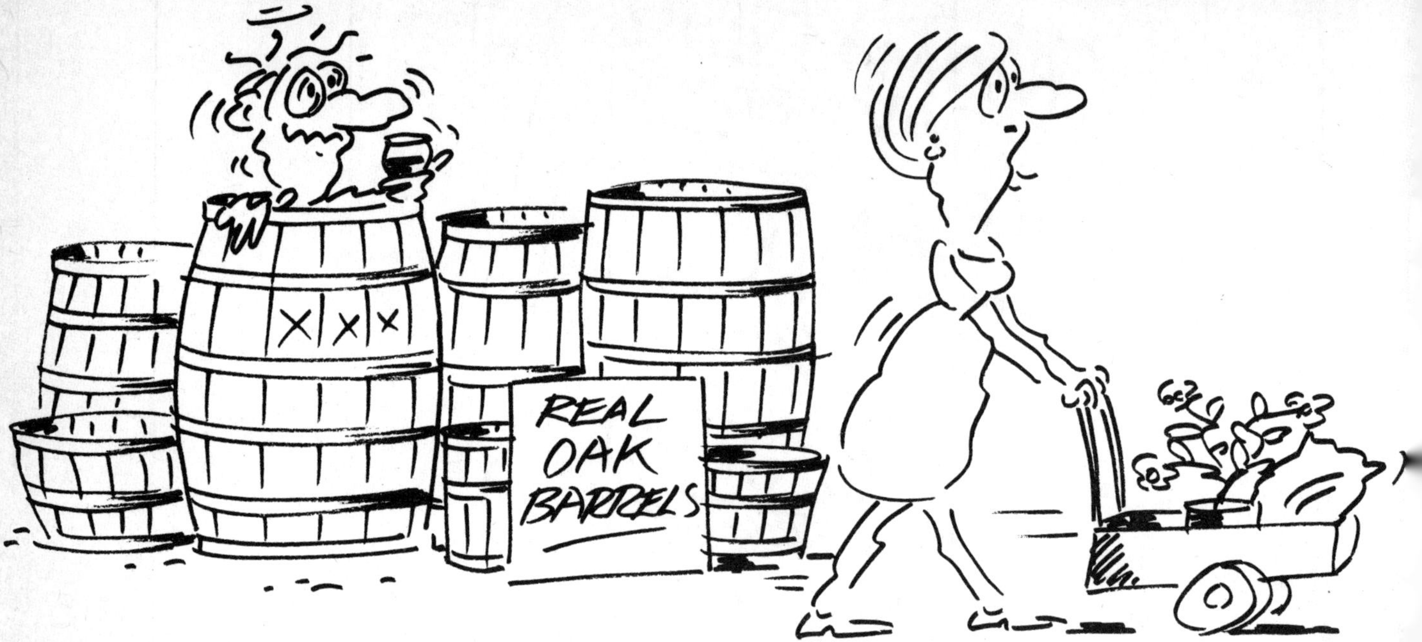
XXX
REAL
OAK
BARRELS

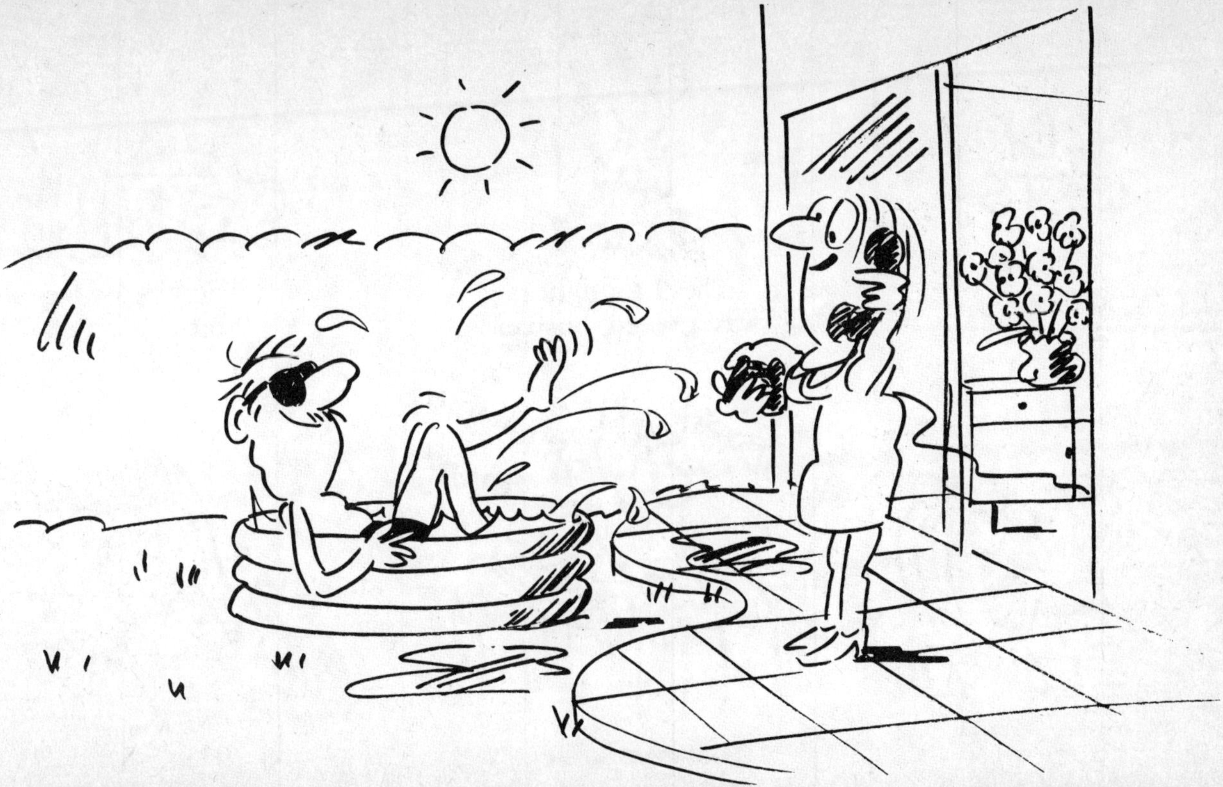

"... that's Andy in our new pool!"

GARDEN PESTS

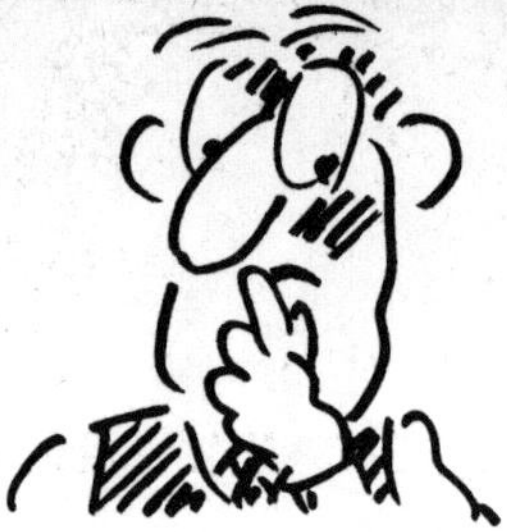

The 'I thought it was a weed' husband

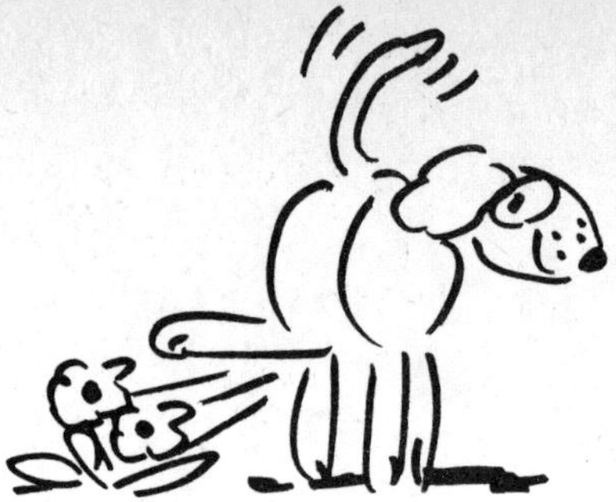

The 'cock-a-leg household pet'

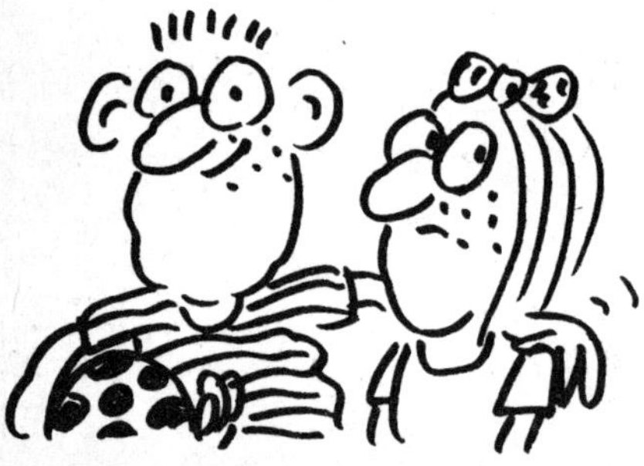

The 'we were only playing' kids

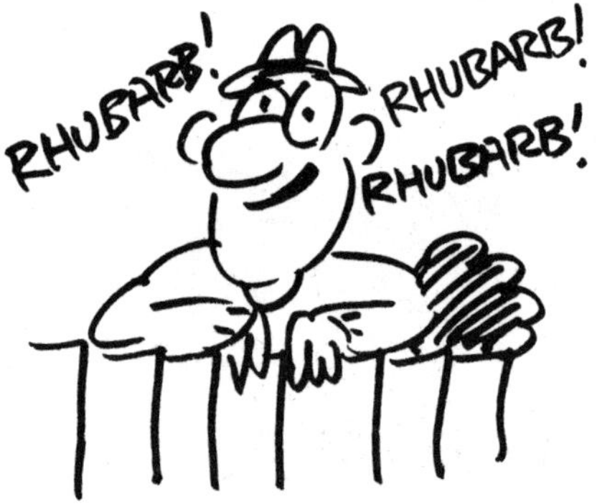
RHUBARB!
RHUBARB!
RHUBARB!
RHUBARB!

The 'ever so helpful man from next door'

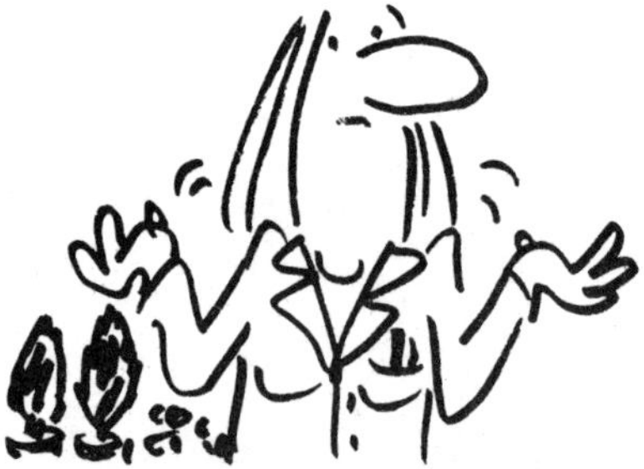

The 'I dunno' garden centre assistant

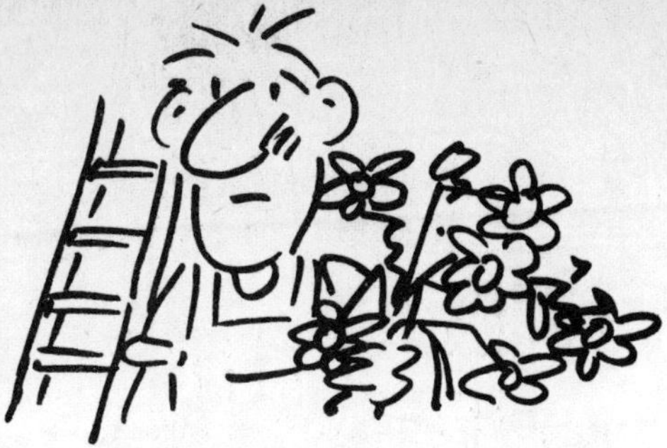

The 'sorry missus I broke these' builder

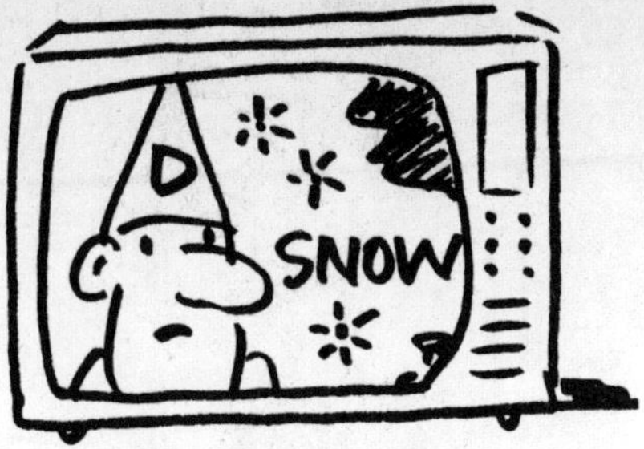
SNOW

The 'well we got it all wrong' weatherman

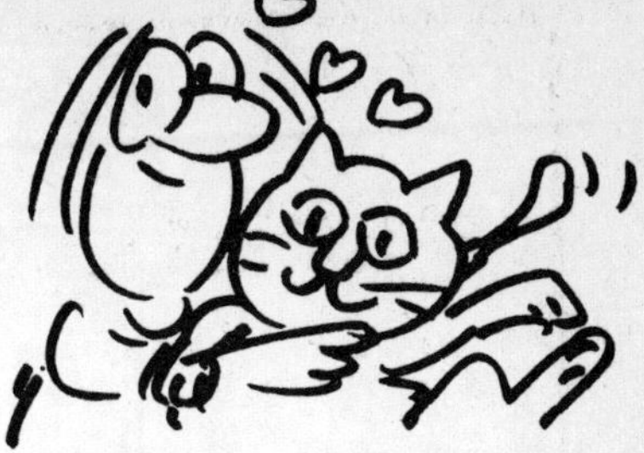

The 'my tiddles wouldn't do that' neighbour

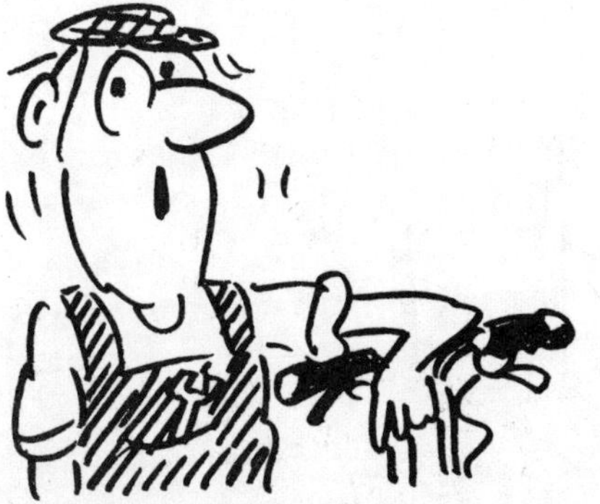

The 'can't do it for three weeks' mower mechanic

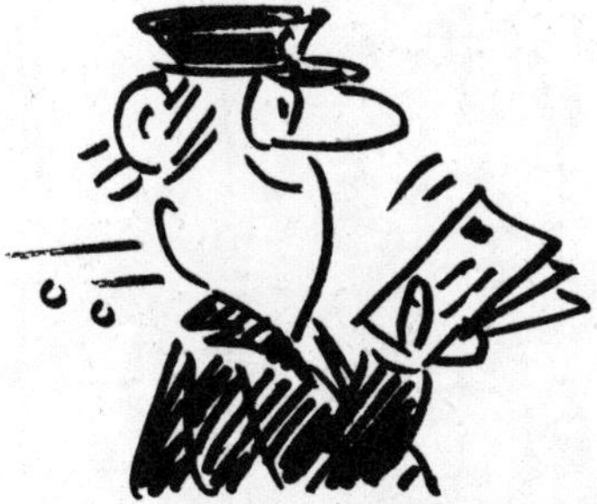

The 'take a shortcut across the lawn' postman

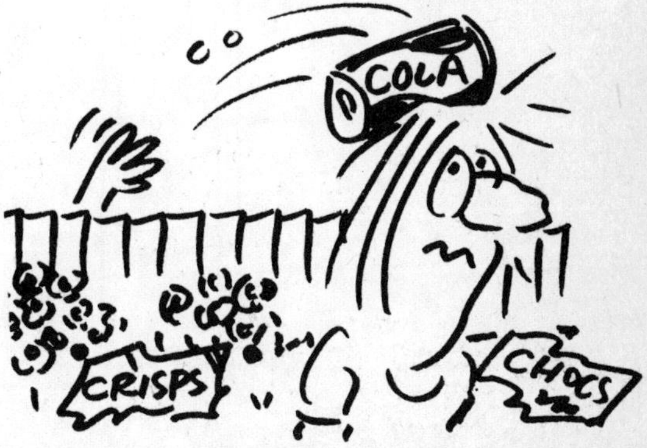
COLA
CRISPS
CHOCS

The 'over the garden wall' litterbug

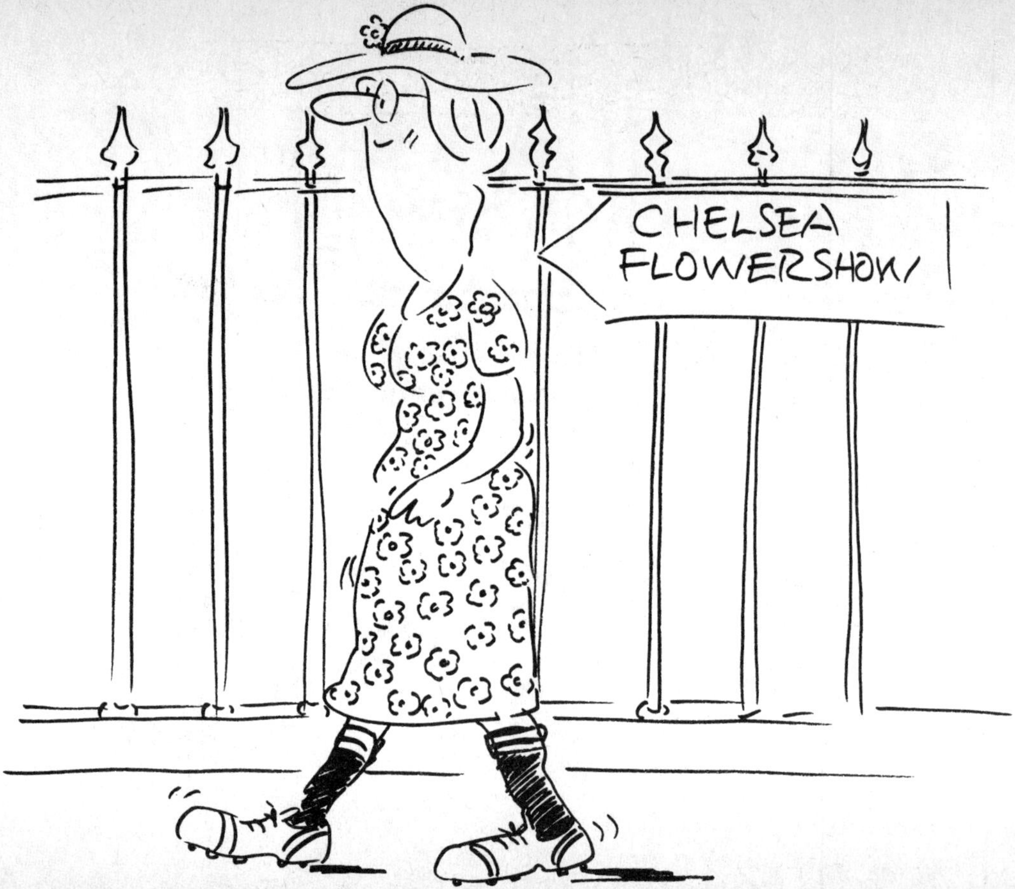
CHELSEA
FLOWERSHOW

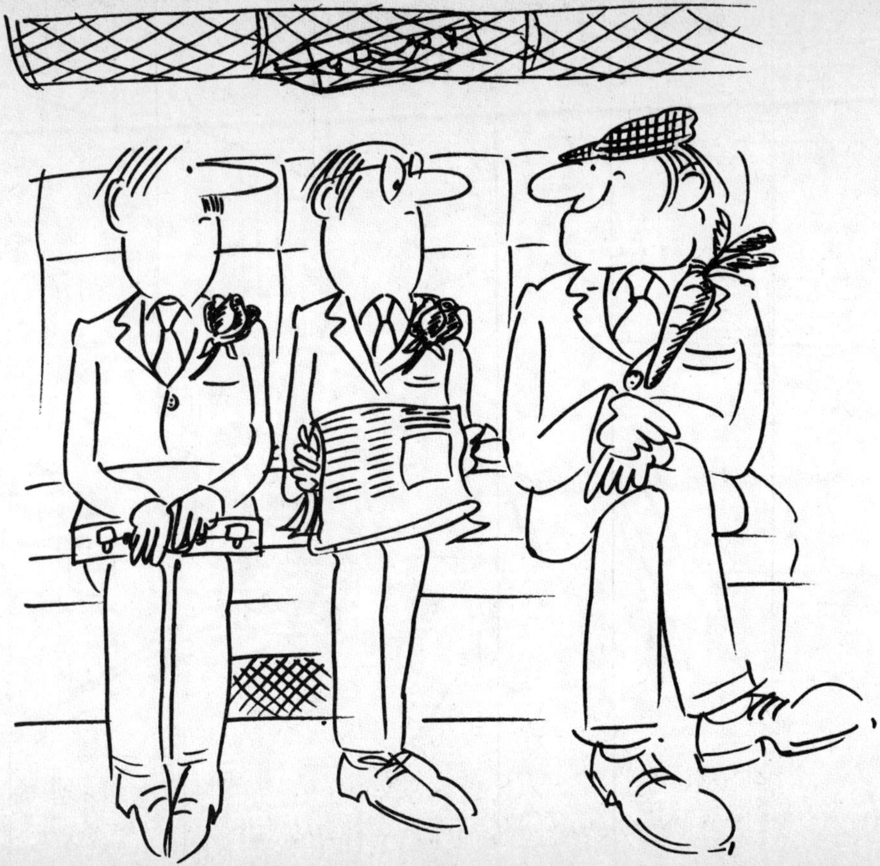

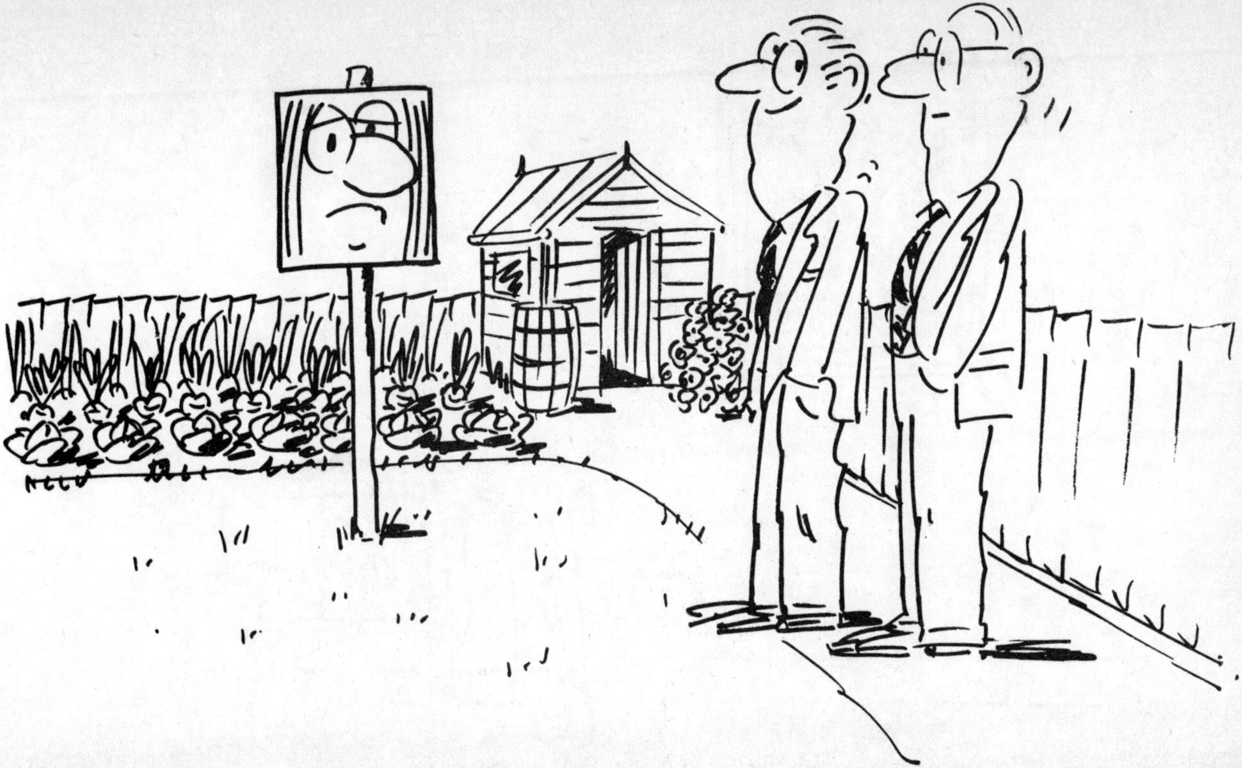

"The mother-in-law, and not a bird in sight!"

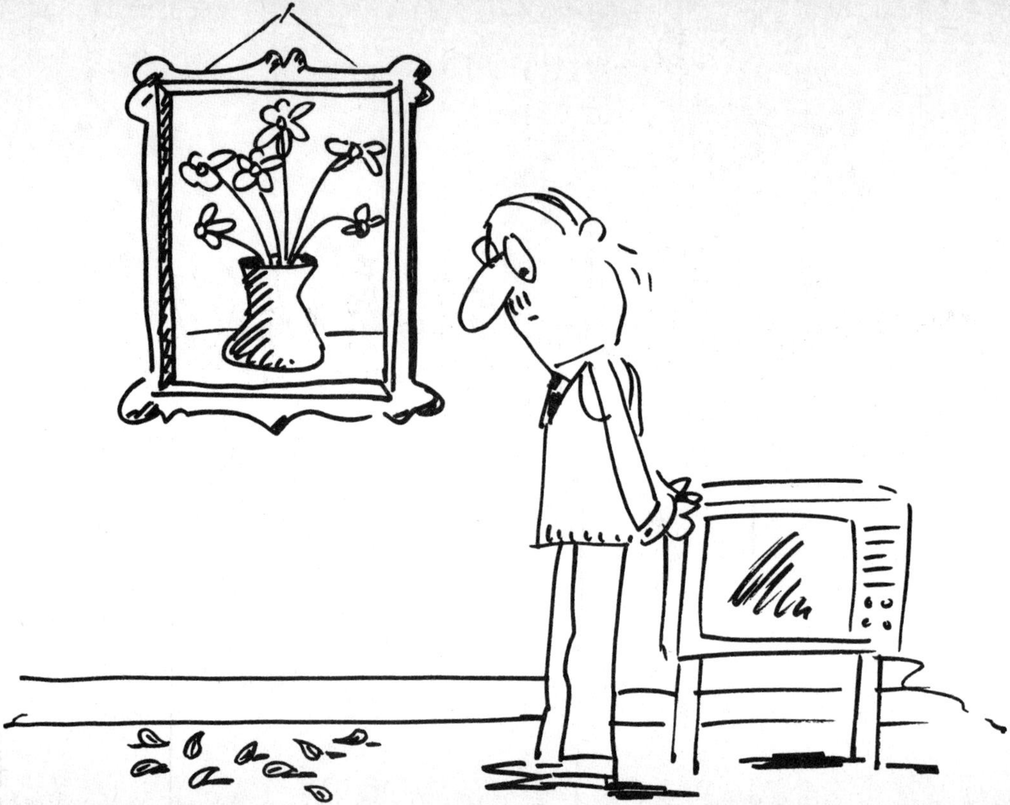

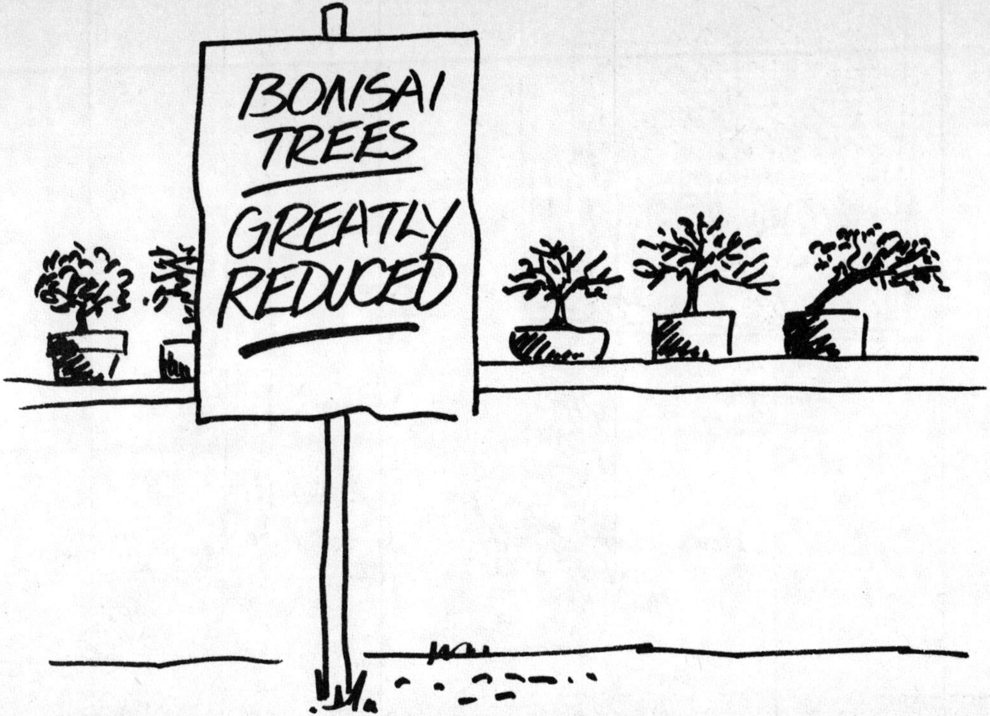
BONSAI TREES
GREATLY REDUCED

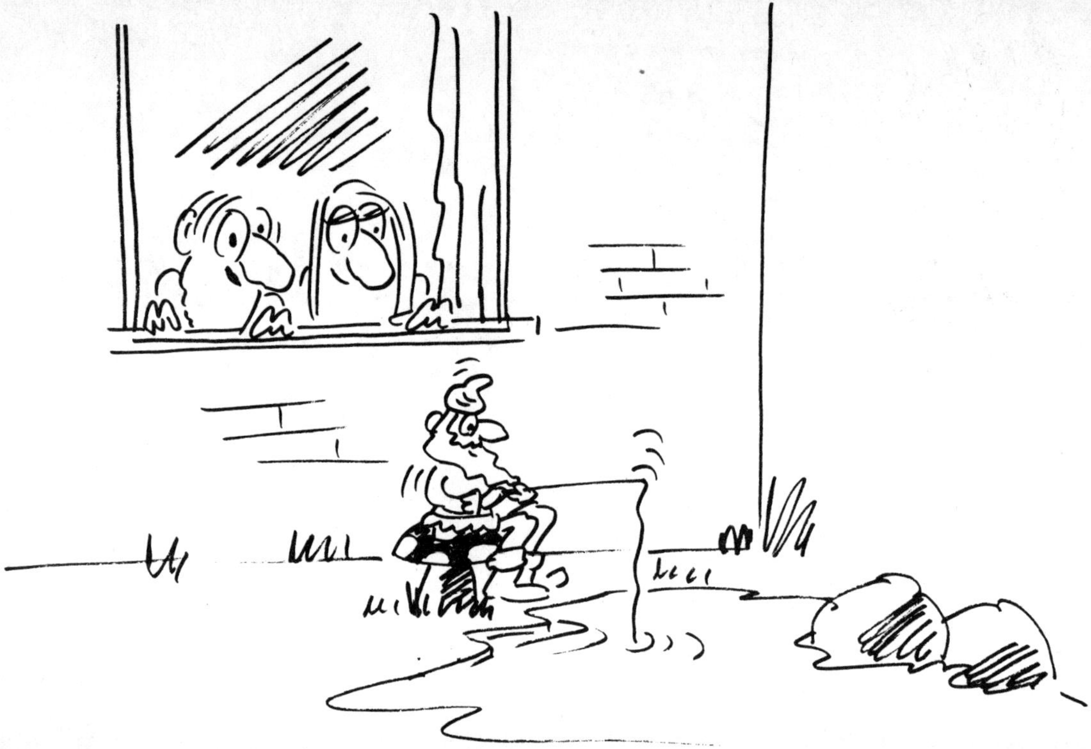

"I think he's got a bite."

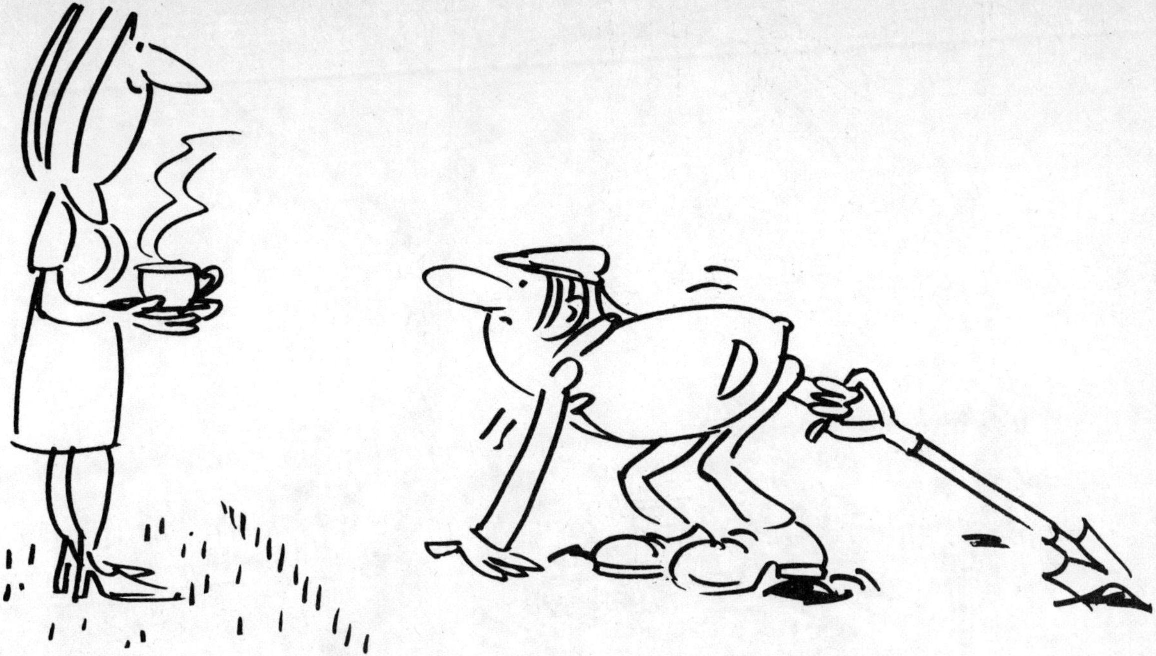

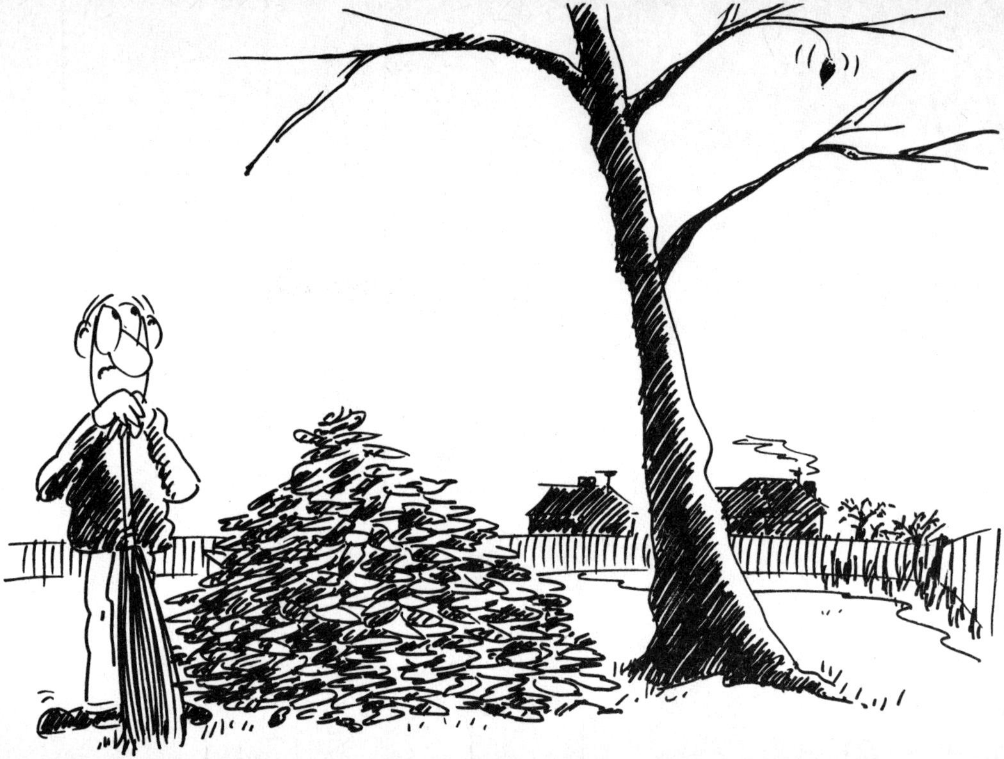

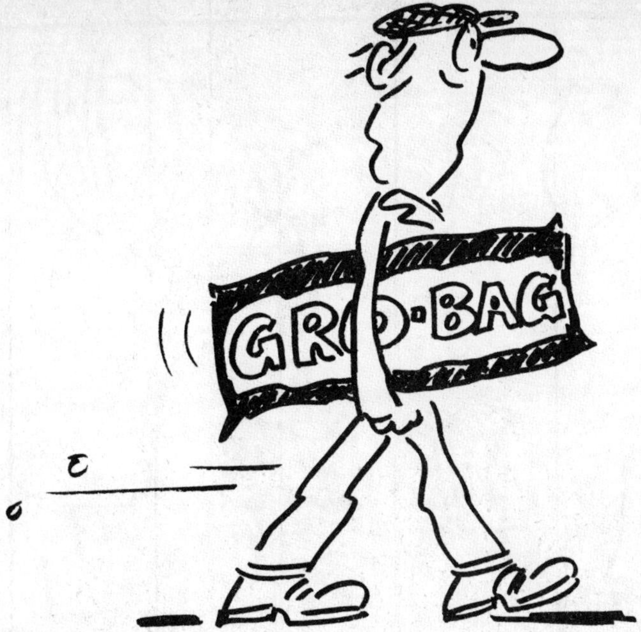
GRO-BAG

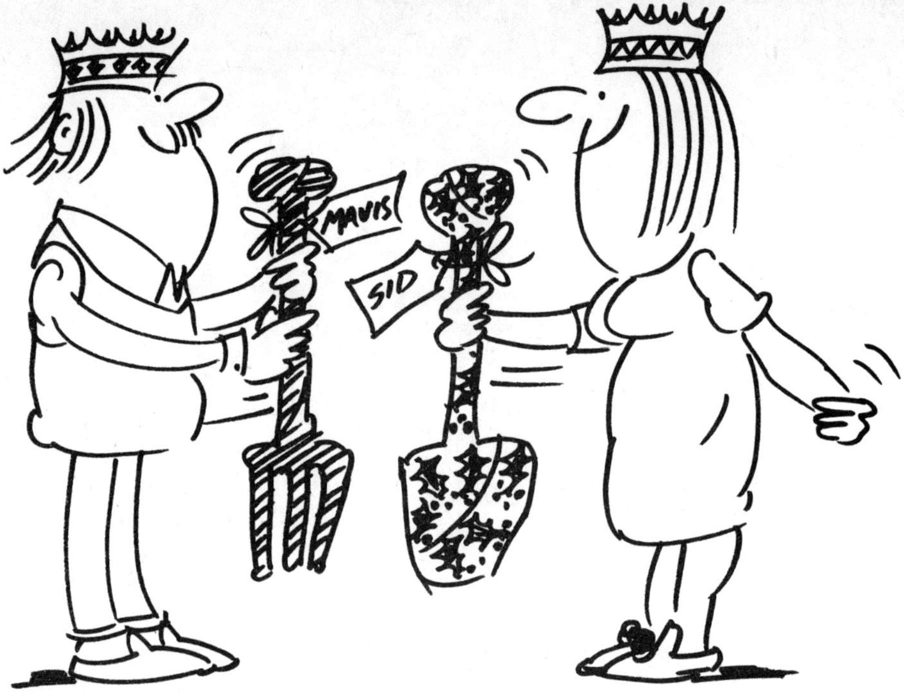
MAVIS
SID

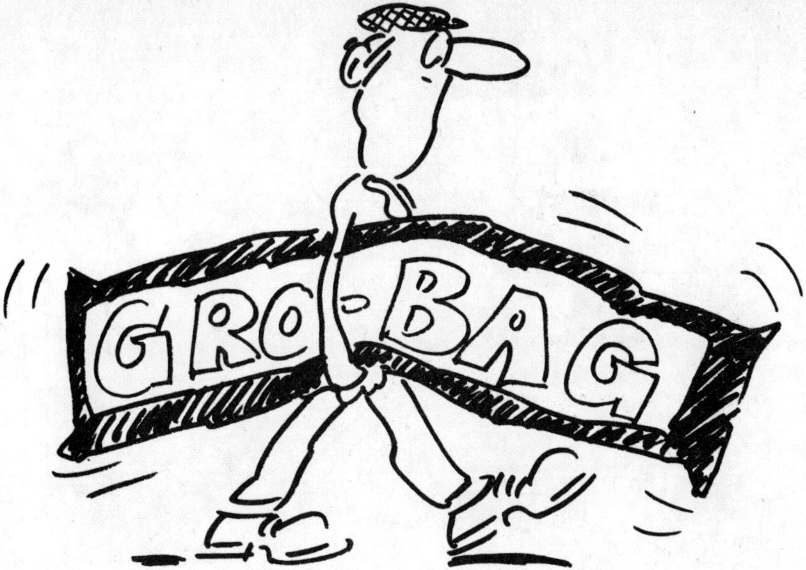
GRO-BAG

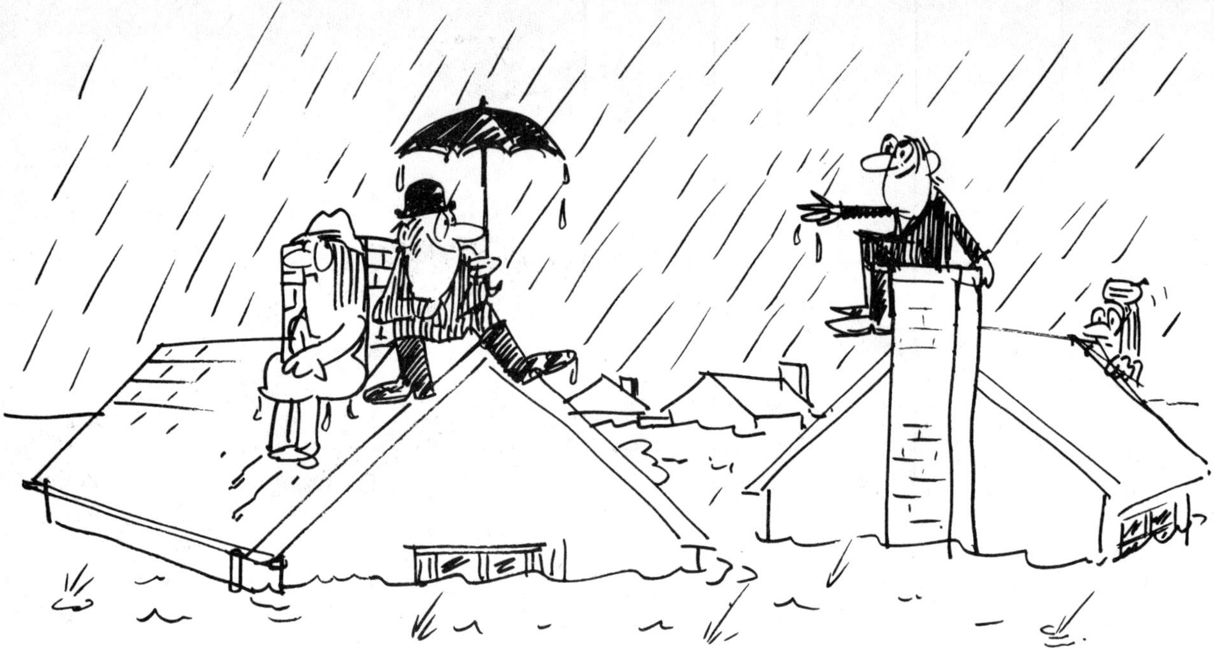

"Good for the garden Roger!"

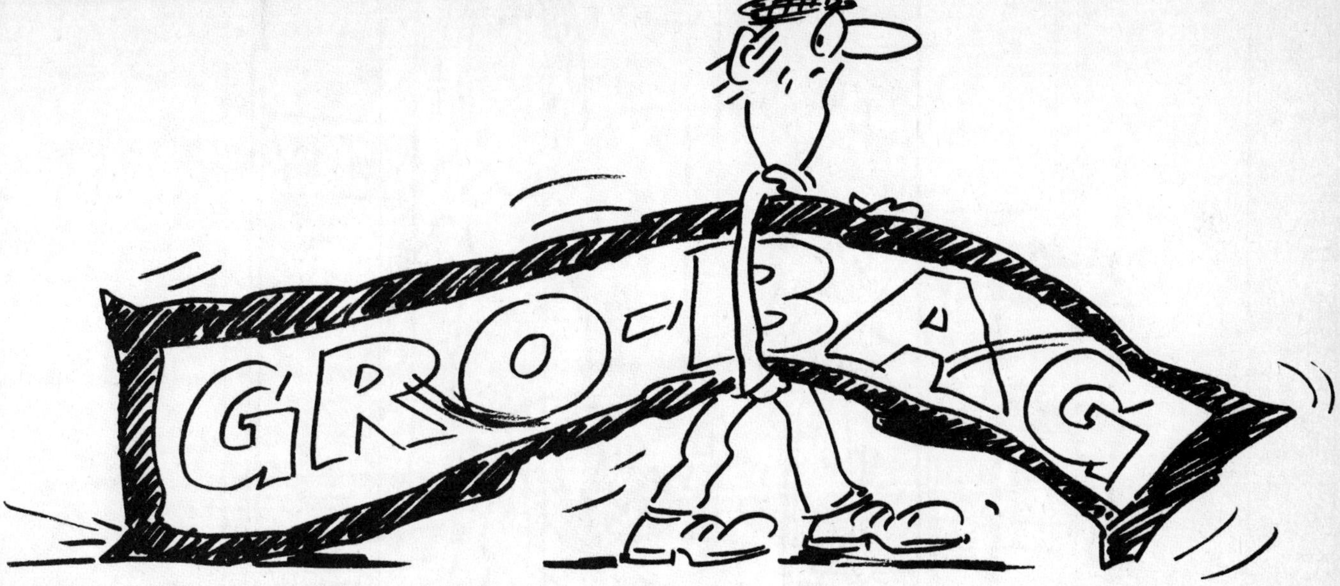
GRO-BAG

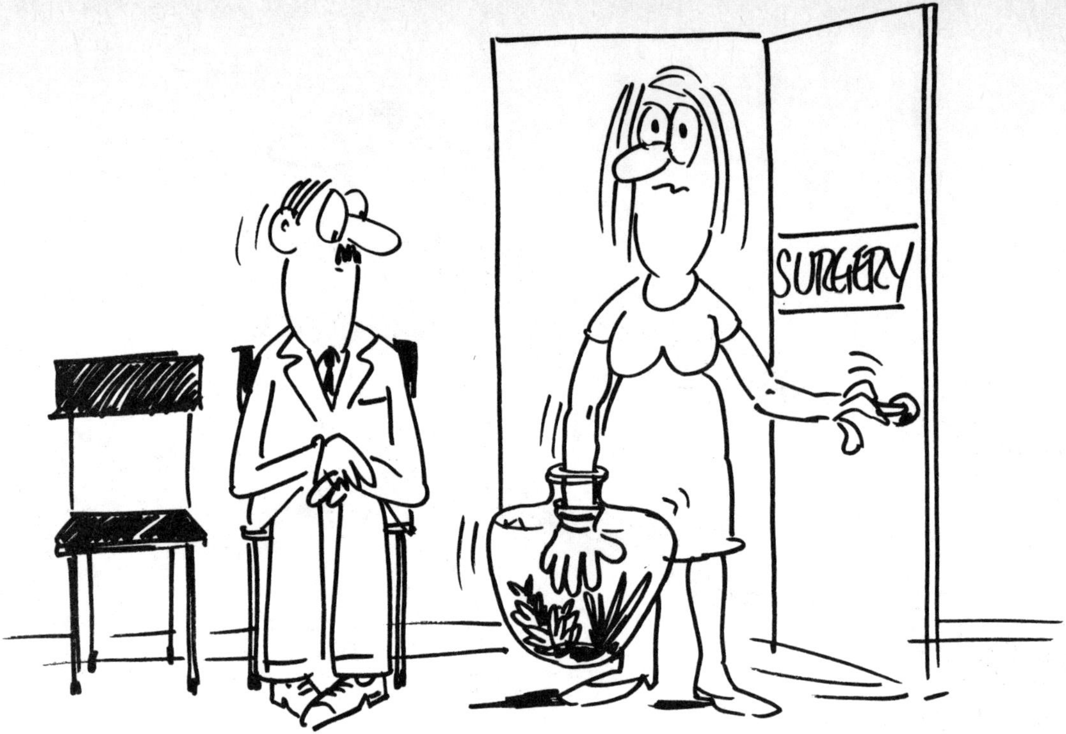
SURGERY

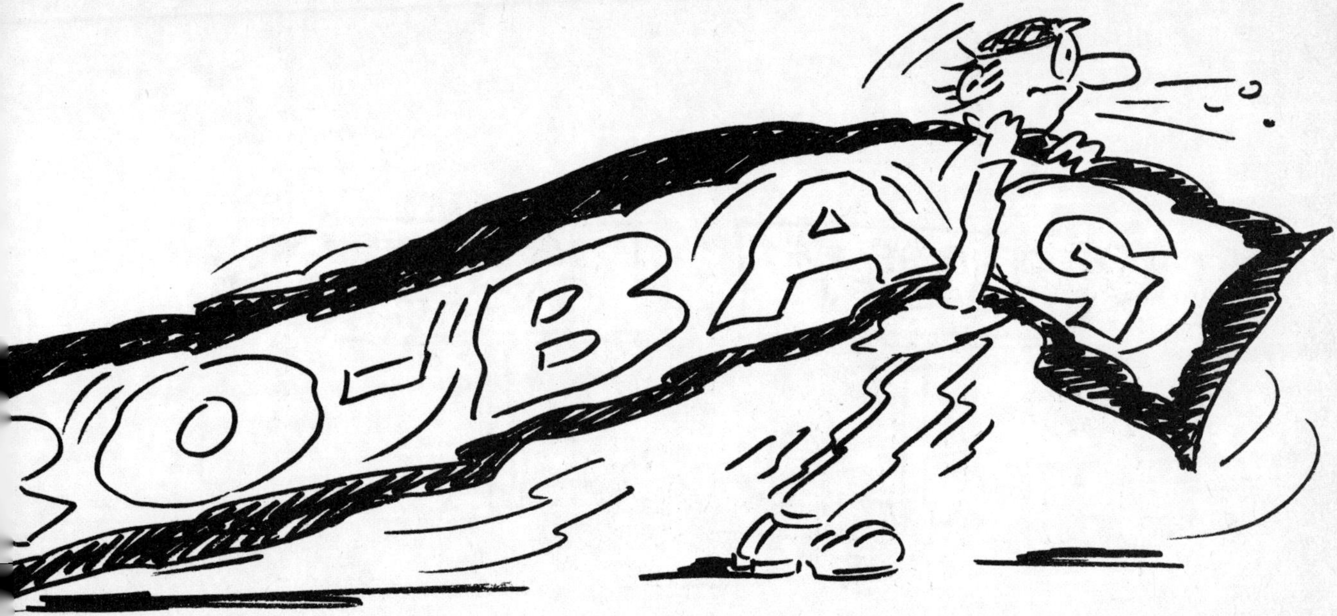
O-BAG

THE SECRET GARDEN
THE SECRET GARDEN

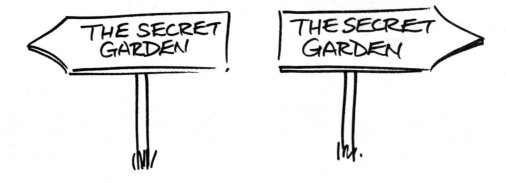

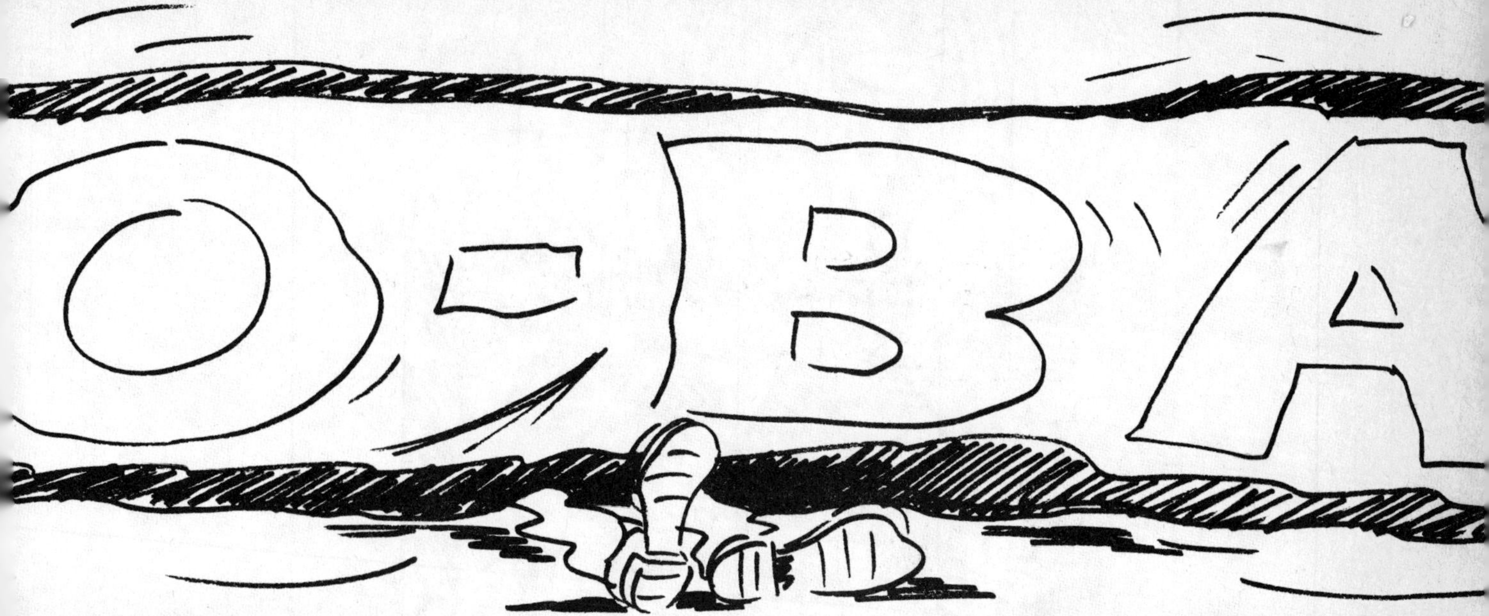
OBA

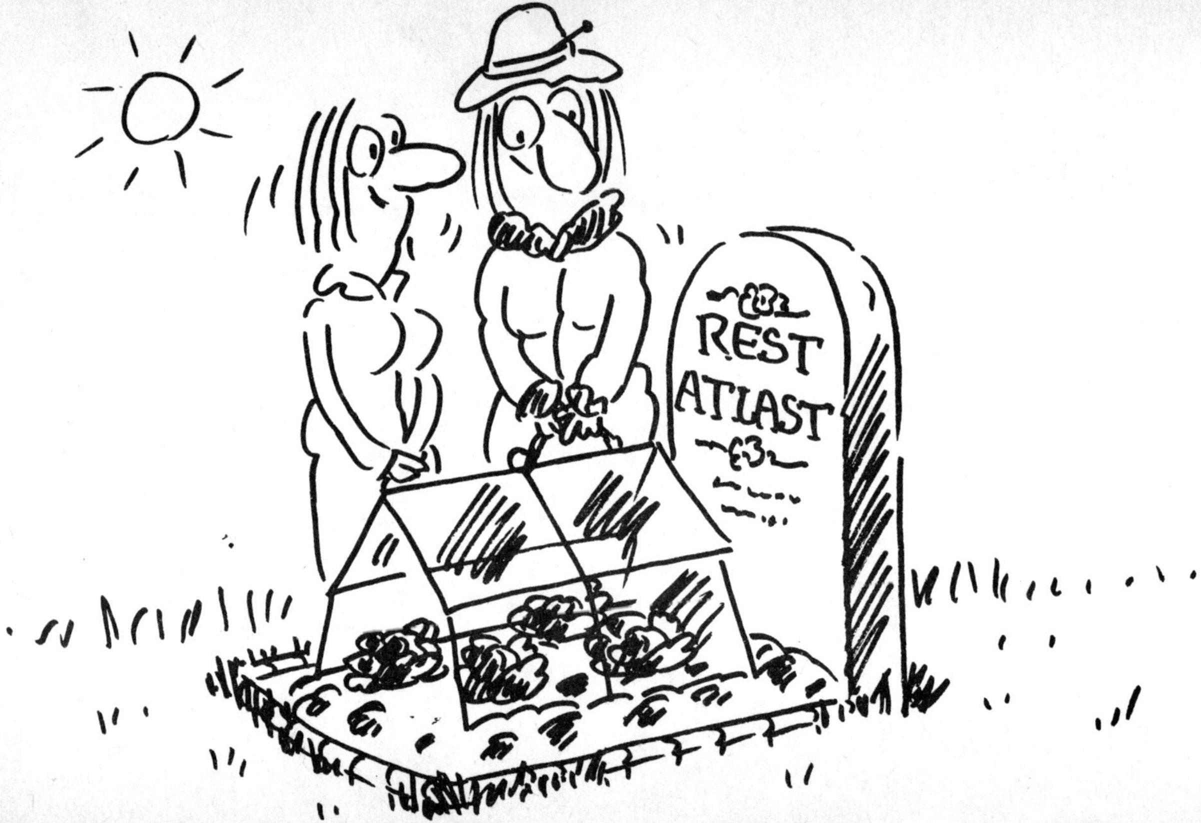
REST
ATLAST

"He always grew lovely lettuces Eve"